TRAVEL REQUIRED:

A Young Man's Journey to Adulthood

DAVE GIBSON

DEDICATION

For Kathi.

CONTENTS

ACKNOWLEDGMENTS

I am grateful to the unknown teacher at Alameda High School who forced me to learn how to type. She helped me more than she could imagine. I am grateful to my parents for letting a 16-year-old venture off absolutely unsupervised on a five-state, 90-day journey with a crew of wheaties. I am deeply grateful to Lisa Crawford for her skillful and patient editing of this book—her work made a substantial difference. I am grateful to Don Dixon Custom Harvesting for my harvesting job in the summer of 1969—it was a remarkably formative summer. I give a special thank you to Ethan Pope for his help in the publishing aspect of this work—he came along at a time when I was absolutely hung up. I am insanely grateful to my assistant Marissa Fuqua who read and corrected the final manuscript, gave me technical expertise and gave me unrelenting accountability at the end of the project. Thank you very much to my niece Lindsay Nelson for reading the final manuscript for typos. Thank you very much to Ken Fuqua, a fellow wheatie, for reading and edits to the final manuscript. Two dozen other people spoke into the process of writing this book over the past 25 years as I worked on the manuscript very part-time and I am grateful to all of them. I am so grateful for my wife Kathi, especially for her patience through this ridiculous process. (Honey, I never meant for this book to take 25 years. Sorry!) Finally, I am most grateful to God for the joy of writing.

Leonardo Da Vinci said, "Art is never finished, only abandoned." Many artists have applied this truth to writing and poetry and film and other art forms. My book is not near as good as anything Da Vinci did and not as it could be, but it is now officially abandoned. Just the same, I wish you would read it.

1 THE JOB BOARD

At sixteen I made a choice I would not understand for decades.

In the spring of 1969 a single sentence written on a three-by-five card led me to my first kiss, my first six pack, my first truck wreck, my first summer away from home, my first brush with the law, and my first anxious taste of freedom. I had no idea how transforming a three-by-five card could be.

The job board at Rapid City Central High School was chaos on cork. Each posting fought for a place, clinging by any little corner in the sea of ads. Most were secured by a thumb tack and skewed at odd angles as job-searching student rotated them in search of a better offer deeper in the chaos. No one managed the board—it just grew. No one approved the ads that went up, and no one removed the ads that expired. The postings quietly grew like layers of wallpaper in an old kitchen.

Like a pearl of great price there may have been a terrific job under the layers, but the job offerings that were visible ranged from child care to painting, street repair to pizza delivery, lawn mowing to roofing, cleaning to selling. They ranged from boring at low pay to mostly boring at a little above low pay. I had already spent a summer washing car windows, another mowing lawns, another as a caddy, another peeling potatoes, and another flipping burgers. This year I was holding out for better.

Rapid City Central High School dominated its block with the big, classic, rectangular high school architecture of the 1920's and 30's: brick, rowed windows, four stories, old steps, straight lines. When I first saw

1

the school as a transfer student from Denver in the fall of 1968, it looked like a prison or an old asylum. It had suffered decades of wear and was beyond the easy fixes of fresh paint and new carpet. The cupped steps, floors shiny with years of wax, and window frames multi-layered with paint were all whimpering, "I am worn tired." What once stood boldly as the pride of the city now seemed to me a factory-like eye sore.

The new high school in Rapid City was overdue and still a year from completion, so in the classrooms, halls, and caféteria of Central High over three thousand students were desperately choked together in a mass that approached human gridlock between class periods. There students were proudly known as "Cobblers."

During his 41 year reign from 1920 to 1961, a coach and athletic director whose last name was Cobb had trained and motivated his various teams to athletic domination in the state of South Dakota. Coach Cobb prevailed to such legendary proportions that the school decided to use his name as the moniker for their mascot.

A cobbler brought to mind the fierce image of a plump, bald, quiet, bespectacled, elderly man clad in a leather apron and bent over a shoe with a very tiny hammer in his hand, a miniature nail in his mouth, and a little tobacco juice seeping from the corner of his mouth. Occasionally he would miss the mark with his nail and say, "Damn." It was enough to strike fear into any opponent.

I combed the job board almost every school day in the search of a new and exciting offering. I was not diligent and never had been, but this search gripped me. As the end of my junior year neared, I needed work and money badly. But even more than money, I needed a taste of life beyond—life beyond my bounded routine of school, sports, church, chores, home, parents, and siblings. I needed to not spend the summer bumming around the house in boredom and resigned to the company of my parents and my younger siblings. For me this was the leading edge of the restless beginnings of launching.

I fantasized that I would find: "Wanted: High School Senior to drive race car for the summer. Excellent pay and benefits. Travel. Room and board provided. No previous experience required. Will train. Driver's license preferred," or, "Wanted: 16-year-old boy to train horses in New Zealand. No previous experience required." These jobs were not on the board—not even buried deep below the pizza delivery openings and the window washing offers.

Knowing there were no exotic jobs, I hoped mostly for a ranch job. Dozens of ranches covered the valleys and hugged edges of the timber around Rapid City. They grew hay in the bottom land and leased forest ground for grazing and fought to put pounds on their cattle. I was scouring the job board for: "Wanted: High school student for summer ranch job. Mending fences, working cattle, building corrals, and other ranch chores. Must have driver's license and be willing to learn to operate machinery. Pay and meals negotiable. Hours will be long." This is what I really wanted. I wanted to drive tractors and buck hay bails and wrestle calves and ride horses through creeks. I wanted to sweat and learn how to stretch fence wire and eat massive suppers. I wanted to spin cookies in old pickups in soggy meadows when the rancher had gone to town for parts. I wanted to break in a cowboy hat.

I wanted to be somebody rough and tumble in the real world. Being a rough and tumble tight end on Friday night was fun. Banging around under the basket against far more talented players had been great and had earned me the reputation for fouling out. I wanted to be physical and competent someplace where there was no referee and no boundary lines. While still lacking discernment there was awareness somewhere in me that I was not going to be much of an athlete. Football and basketball would soon be a thing of the past for me. College athletics was out of the question for a guy who ran the hundred-yard-dash in about an hour. However vague these athletic realizations were, they were driving me on to the next thing in my young life.

Like the race car job, the ranch posting never materialized. I was sure that ranch workers were more needed than race car drivers. I did not understand—did not even have a clue—that ranchers do not bring little, neatly printed, three-by-five cards to high school job boards. Ranchers who needed help talked to their neighbors and friends. They were hiring their children, their nephews or their neighbor's kids. For the first of many times I did not know the right people. I knew I worked a whole lot harder than the average nephew, but I was not the son of Mr. Rancher's little sister. Mr. Rancher had never heard of me, and he never would hear of me because I limited my job search to the tornado of postings in the hallway of Rapid City Central. But it was the only place I knew to look, my only idea.

One noon, my hope waning, I skipped lunch to scour the board again. A new ad had appeared—freshly tacked on top of the matted mess. It was hand written on a three-by-five card. "Wanted: Custom wheat harvesters. Travel required. Must have driver's license. No previous experience necessary." The message hooked something in me. Decades later I would understand that I was captured not so much by the kind of work as by two words: "Travel required." What I did not yet know was that I was a sojourner, a pioneer, an adventurer, a vagabond, a high-plains drifter. Genetically I had inherited this bent from my father. Environmentally, I had been towed by him around the western states for my entire 16 years—now already living in my eighth town.

"Travel required" meant adventure and seeing country that I had not seen. It meant that I got to do something unique and off-beat that no one else at school would do and that would give me bragging rights when I got back in the fall. It meant not taking my little sisters to their piano lessons and not lobbying with my parents for every little request or plan that was out of our well bounded routine. It meant freedom and self-supervision which was for me, as for most 16-year-olds, no measurable supervision at all.

With the travel wiring inside me and my special gift for falling in love instantly, I already wanted this job. The chance of my parents letting me take it seemed small. Anxiety rose up in me. It felt like aching for the cheerleader to say, "Yes, I'll go out with you," all the while knowing that she will say no. I had a "gift" for wanting deeply what I was not going to get—for making everything in life intense and draining. It was a gift which made my childhood and adolescence markedly more anxious than most.

I wrote down the name and phone number on the card. I did not need to write down any details; they were already logged in my memory. I drove my father's yellow, rag-top Bronco the 28 miles home—west out of Rapid City, through Nemo, three more miles on the pavement, left onto the gravel road, across the cattle guard into Boxelder Job Corps Center, up the hill to the end of the dirt road, and left into our driveway.

I drove this route morning and evening five days a week. I knew it so well that I occasionally frightened myself by "coming to" just as I turned off the pavement onto the Job Corps Center road—arriving 28 miles from where I left school and having never registered along the way the open stands of Ponderosa Pine, hills, tourist traps, cabins, Forest Service trail signs, bridges, hitch hikers, hay fields, "wide-spot-in-the-road" stores, cattle, abandoned vehicles, potholes, or traffic. While driving home from football or basketball practice the familiarity of the route lulled me to some unknown place. That familiarity combined with the low, rhythmic slapping of the cloth top of my Dad's Bronco would cast a spell on my tired teenage mind.

By the time the Bronco rested on the gravel driveway, I had my pitch ready. I had rehearsed the presentation, enumerated the benefits, arranged the points in their most marketable order, and found reasonable answers for probable objections. This was a big chance for a small-town boy to break out into the bigger world. It was a chance to be myself separate from Dad and Mom and the kids and the known things that had defined my life for 16 years. These things were not so much bad things as rapidly becoming past things. I was 16, the oldest of five children, and living in what I perceived to be a tightly controlled household. I was tired of it all—the routines and the control and the place I held in the family system. My "place" could roughly be defined as dominated by Dad, distant from Mom and alternately resented, ignored, tolerated or put upon by my siblings. It is not fair to say that they did not care about me, and it is not fair to say that our family life was miserable. It is not fair to say that there were not fun times. However, it is both fair and accurate to say that I was deeply infected with the virus to leave.

This chance for a three-month foray into independent life must be managed with care. If I failed in my pitch I would be logging another summer of family Sunday drives, odd chores, and many forms of boredom in and around Nemo. If I succeeded I was off on a great adventure. "Travel required," the card had said and that was in rhythm with my soul.

Like most 16-year-olds I was an expert on selling ideas to my parents. Once inside our government-issue three-bedroom, one-bath ranch house, I sized up the clients and the sales environment.

My mom was cooking supper. Like her mother before her Mom was a working machine—cooking, cleaning, sewing, gardening, parenting, and whatever needed doing. She was a good, methodical cook who had long since stopped using recipes. The menu did not vary much but it was tasty and plentiful. For breakfast she rotated between scrambled eggs, pancakes, French toast, cold cereal and oatmeal. Lunch shifted between baloney or grilled cheese sandwiches, hamburgers, tomato or potato soup, and macaroni and cheese. At supper we ate a big meal of tacos or spaghetti or meatloaf or pot roast with potatoes or fried chicken or "clean out the fridge" casseroles. On the good days we got seven-layer salad or cinnamon rolls or homemade bread or sour-cream brownies.

My siblings were in their rooms and occupied with the kinds of things that captivate kids in 1969. It would be unheard of for any of us siblings to leave our rooms or activities to welcome another sibling home. Between the five of us there was too little mutual interest and too much going out and coming in home to jump up every time the door opened.

My Dad was not yet home from his work as the director of the

Boxelder Job Corps Center. He may be listening to an angry employee or giving an "attitude adjustment interview" to a corpsman, or walking around to see what was working and what was not. This job was his latest assignment in a long string of US Forest Service moves—California to South Dakota to Wyoming to Colorado back to South Dakota. "Travel required."

I could make an initial pitch to my Mom in the hope of swaying her early. In this particular case this was a risky approach. Mom was usually the easier sell, and conventional wisdom said to get her "OK" before Dad had wind of my outrageous plan. However, this request seemed too big to pull this trick. It appeared to me that Dad held the only vote on really important issues in our home, making them always either 1-0 or 0-1. One way or another it was going to be unanimous and there was no margin for error. I could have been wrong. Maybe my mother had more say that I thought. I decided to hold my appeal until Dad was also home and pitch it in one big, risky roll of the tongue.

I retreated to my room which my younger brother and I shared, as teenage boys will, in relative squalor. Telling us to clean our room was about on par with telling us to sweep the forest—it may be a good idea but it was too much work for mere mortals. It was not dirty in the unsanitary sense because Mom took care of all of that. It was only dirty in the utter clutter and chaos sense. We did not often put clothes away—it would take too much energy. We did not put books or sporting goods in any order or place—it would require too much discipline. We did not make any effort to decorate the room—it never crossed our minds. So the net result was unmade beds and a floor so cluttered that we could hardly walk on the carpet.

Every piece of furniture in our room- the bunk beds, the dresser, the study desk, and the two locking footlockers- were built by my grandfather. My mother's dad, Grandpa Fred Bierman, had been stricken with some disease that robbed from him the ability to walk. He built large, utilitarian, plywood furniture in his driveway or in his garage, sawing 4 by 8 sheets of plywood with a hand saw while seated in a kitchen chair.

On that anxious day, before I made my pitch, I put my books on the study desk and left them there, as was my habit, unopened. The desk saw no actual use for study though it was used extensively for piling. My brother did not need to study owing to his intellect. I did not need to study owing to my laziness. It was the one way that we were alike: neither one of us really needed a desk. "Great dread" is the only way to describe the thought of opening a book, reading it, taking notes on it and attempting to retain something of use. My folks had given up trying to make me do it, and I was personally unable to do it. I regretted it even then. I only did enough to get passable grades and called it good. An utter lack of self-discipline was another "gift"of my youth.

When Dad got home, I acted as normal as I was able. Dad may not have known exactly what was coming but he probably suspected that something was coming. Dad had by this time been on the receiving end of uncounted "major sales pitches" by his children. He could see through a looming sales pitch like a freshly scrubbed window. My fear was always that he would judge the pitch before I had made my case.

When Mom called us that evening we sat down for dinner in our given places. Our kitchen table landed in so many different houses that we found some sense of place and stability by sticking to our given seats around the table. The reasons for our positions were no longer known, except for my brother's place at the opposite end from my Dad. My brother was a picky eater and immediately rebelled against food being put on his plate by my father. Being a very willful child in his own way, my brother homesteaded the chair most distant from Dad and thus most distant from the possibility of getting unacceptable food items on his plate, or worse yet, from getting food co-mixed on his plate. Alan believed that your stomach had separate compartments for each different food and he would not eat things that were mixed together. He ate each item separately—in a precise, if unexplainable, order.

We prayed our family prayer in the unison and perfection that we had achieved over the years. Were there a competition for "synchronized praying" in the Olympics we were gold. "Come Lord Jesus be our Guest and let these gifts to us be blessed. Amen. Please pass the potatoes." For the longest time my little sister thought "Please pass the potatoes" was simply the end of the prayer.

A request to spend the entire summer away and unsupervised was audacious. But it was also dicey because my parents were the veterans of five children. They had developed a "sales resistance" that automatically steered to "no," and required unusual skill to move the needle to "yes." Years of requests that my parents deemed to be immature, foolish, and selfish had jaded them. If I could get Dad away from "no" and over to "I'll think about it" I would have a major foothold. There would be some hope.

This sales setting was especially difficult because my siblings where present. They were unpredictable at best and unkind at worst. My brother trailed behind me by 20 months and three younger sisters were spattered over the next eight years behind him. Any one of the four could say something, innocently or maliciously, that would sabotage my plan. They might raise any number of objections—authentic and manufactured. If they were angry at me for some past sin or imagined injustice, they might oppose my idea simply for reasons of retaliation.

I was well aware that they were usually part of the setting in these kinds of sales. It was just part of the playing field. All siblings understood it. Nothing could be done, and there was really no predicting which way these four players would go in the discussion. If anyone of them harmed this sale they would pay for it at a later time. As I began my pitch, they seemed to sense the great value of this idea to me and therefore opted for silence.

I began my pitch in as subtle and nonchalant a manner as possible, which is to say that I blurted out my plan. I began not because I felt the timing was right but because I could not hold it any longer.

"Dad," I started, "I was looking at the job board at lunch and I found a job driving a wheat combine for the summer. Do you think I could take it?" I revealed only the basics and none of the details. I let it rest there. My thinking was that it might sound good to him and dispose him to move a little off of "no" before I had to reveal other details of the proposition.

"That might be good." He responded.

So far, so good. I hesitated, hoping he would say more. When he did not say more I was forced to go on.

"It said that you needed a driver's license but no experience," I offered.

Dad replied, "Well, whose farm would you be driving on? I can't guarantee that you can have the Bronco all summer." He was thinking far enough down the road to even ask where I would be working. It was a good sign.

"I wouldn't need the Bronco at all, Dad. I would travel with this custom harvester from Oklahoma up to Montana and cut wheat all the way up," I said.

When the true nature of the request was revealed, the fact that I wouldn't be tying up his Bronco seemed inconsequential and really did nothing to tip the scales in my favor. A whole summer out in farm country rubbing shoulders with hellions and scarcely supervised by a wheat harvester was a whole different proposition than working for a guy eighteen miles down the road, a guy whom my father could call to brief on my boundaries and check on my performance.

A "new-to-our-family" reality enveloped our kitchen. Many

appeals had been made in the past dozen years around this table. Some were common garden variety requests like sleep-overs and new toys. Some were wild like getting your own room and putting the other four siblings in one room. But these were cards no one had ever played at this table. They were cards no one had considered. Our family had not felt this tension before. We knew the tensions of anger and of anxiety and of indifference. Now a new realization dawned on all of us.

As a family we were on the edge of spreading out.

This emotionally distant but physically close band of seven people had traveled together through six Western states, multiple towns in those states, and uncounted houses in those towns. Now the seven of us were, for the first serious time, forced to face the reality that we were not going to be together forever and indeed not for long.

We were comfortable with each other and loved each other with the kind of love our generation knew. We did not hug or kiss or say, "I love you," but we did get along mostly, and reset after fights and generally got through life together. We did have the unspoken covenant of blood relations and the visceral instinct to stick together. The US Forest Service, with some previous help from the Border Patrol and the Federal Predator Program, had made gypsies of us and ingrained in our collective identity the belief that we were fellow sojourners and that it was, more often than not, us against the world. We never stopped long enough to reflect on that reality and decide if we liked roaming. However, we were certainly accustomed to it.

Unlike the other propositions and pitches that came across this table to Dad and Mom, no one knew immediately if they liked it or not. That in itself was a strange feeling—to not have an immediate response. My siblings were surprised. By their standards and expectations I was clearly out of the envelope of reasonable requests; however, they could not see an immediate objection. The request was so unusual that they apparently weren't sure if they liked the idea, and if they didn't like it they weren't sure how to object. Perhaps for the first time it occurred to them that we would not always live here in this house or in some house together, that we would not forever occupy these self-assigned seats, and that their oldest brother would naturally be the first to fly. Each one sat and ate and processed the idea that their brother might not be home all summer long, the idea that their brother would not be policed for when to be home, bed times, choice of friends and drinking beer or smoking was more than they could process.

My parents were surprised and clearly not prepared for this idea. Although, it seemed that they were not as opposed to it as I thought they might have been. The idea was naked on the table and still alive. I let it lie there and fight for life like a premature baby sucking hard into underdeveloped lungs. It was clearly too early to begin answering objections. I had ruined other sales by answering objections before they were raised. It was an amateur mistake and I was not going to make it with an idea this valuable. If I said more right now, I might help it and I might not.

"We'll think about it," Dad said at last. To keep the idea breathing this long was a victory. I let it rest. I prayed it would live out the night. *Let the baby fight for precious life and don't kill it with even the hint of pressure*, I told myself. Dad would think about it and get a read from Mom about it.

I would think about it too. The possibility oscillated wildly in me like the terrific excitement of something fully unknown and semi-frightening, but something you nevertheless want very badly. I would be without family or friends. I would be free to shape my relationships and bound to defend myself. I would be free to spend my own money and bound to pay my own bills. I would be free to stay out all hours and bound to be battered by the fatigue. I would be free to make my own choices and bound to suffer my own consequences. This was all filtering into me. I became obsessed with the possibility and all the ideas that swirled around it.

The next day I called the number to get more details. The local contact was a college student named Mark Wheeler from the Black Hills School of Mines. Mark had worked for the harvester before. As the crew supervisor, he was trying to find local students to join the summer crew.

Mark told me that Don Dexter, the harvester, had a farm in Alva, Oklahoma where he raised a few cows and a lot of wheat, but he also had four combines, four two-ton trucks, two one-ton trucks that pulled two trailer houses and a pickup. Dexter took this aging and un-matched train of harvest machinery on the road every summer from southern Oklahoma all the way to southern Alberta. Dexter and his cobbled-together crew followed the wheat harvest as it ripened, easing along in the thin band of ripening wheat as it edged north. At every stop Dexter cut wheat for previous customers and for new customers if he could find them. In Alva he cut his own wheat, stored it in the co-op, and moved on north.

Mark continued by telling me that Dexter paid his harvesters $1.50 an hour when the combines were cutting and $0.75 an hour when the combines were being moved. He needed four guys to drive combines and four guys to drive trucks while Dexter himself took care of the billing, parts running, repairs, supervising, and, I was to learn, the chasing of every available woman when his wife was not around. Mrs. Dexter and three grade school kids were reluctant passengers on this ragged harvest train as it jerked and stopped and lumbered from south to north. Don's wife cooked, his kids whined, and Don ignored them all.

"Don Dexter is eager to hire you," Mark assured me. What Mark did not tell me, and my parents must have known, was that the men and boys who worked the custom wheat harvest were un-affectionately known to local farmers and merchants as "wheaties." As it turned out, if you had a pulse and could drive you were qualified to be a wheatie for Don Dexter. No one was going to look at your driver's license, check your police record or ask for any references. The bar was not high; near the end of the summer it would get lower. There was no application form but had there been one it would have simply read, "Do you have a pulse and if so when can you start?"

In most farm towns wheaties were the agricultural equivalent of carnival workers, panhandlers, drifters and bums. I did not have a clue about the ranks I might be joining. I would learn that many of them were unreliable, often dishonest, opportunistically untrustworthy, and generally ragged people. They were prone to leave a given crew with the smallest provocation and with the smallest notice, or with no notice at all. When leaving for another crew or for another town, they would often take anything of value that was not bolted to a truck or physically in the bosses' hand. Many of them were given to hard drinking, tired women, chain smoking, fist fighting, and gambling away advances of money that they had not yet even earned. When the wheaties were in town farmers generally shipped their daughters to grandma's, kept their sons in sight, and locked their tool sheds.

When I was making this pitch to my parents, I did not know any of this. They must have known some part of it, if not all of it. My mother was raised on a farm in South Dakota and my father had been in the US Army Air Corps during World War II. Dad had also worked as a government trapper on sheep ranches in South Dakota and served in the US Border Patrol in Presidio, Texas. They had to know the kind of setting I was asking to spend the summer in. Given everything they knew that I did not know, it was amazing that my idea lived the night.

That next day school went well except track practice was, as usual, long and miserable. I was one of the "weight men" on our highly rated track team. I threw the discus and did it poorly. The track team's distance guys were in the top of the pack and our sprinters were the best in the region; however, our shot putters and discus throwers were scattered between fair and embarrassing. I was anchoring the embarrassing end of the athletic spectrum. I was not a track man. I did well in football, held my own in basketball, wished we had baseball, and stunk in track. But I went out for track because I was a jock, and this was the only sport in the spring. It was one of those horrible examples of path dependency—blindly staying in your rut—that a person regrets for a long time.

We stretched, ran, and practiced our technique in the discus. My personal technique amounted to spinning around several times, throwing the heavy rubber plate with a last-instant, arm-searing, tendon-stretching, finger-popping, pain-inducing burst of energy, and then attempting not to scratch. The only part I really had perfected was the arm injuring part. The spinning and not scratching parts still needed work. In a dual meet out at the local Air Force base I had placed fourth out of five kids, which allowed me to letter in track. It was my only throw in competition over 140 feet. In the state meet, long after I had been eliminated, I marked the national record throw by a kid from Brookings who went over 200 feet. Track for me was one of my many personal exercises in endurance. I saved face by not quitting.

When practice mercifully ended that day, I showered, jumped in the Bronco and set west for home. My mind was loaded with reasons, additional ammunition, and benefits of cutting wheat for Don Dexter. I rearranged the second round of my presentation a dozen times on the trip home.

Again Dad was not home and again I opted to leave the question alone until he was. When he did get home I couldn't wait for the dinner table and suffer the audience of my siblings.

"Dad, what do you think about my idea of the harvesting job?" I asked as soon as he set down his satchel.

"Well, I think I need to know some more about it," was his answer. "What else do you know about this job?"

I was eager to tell him and I took hope in even getting to fill in the details. "I know the crew starts in southern Oklahoma and goes all the way to Montana cutting wheat. They have four combines and I would live in the crew trailer. They pay $1.50 when you are cutting wheat and 75 cents when you are just moving the equipment. The foreman also said that I could start as soon as school is out."

"You talked to the foreman?" Dad asked.

"Yes," I said, "I called him on the phone and asked him a bunch of stuff."

"Who is the foreman?" Dad wanted to know.

"He is a college kid in Rapid City named Mark. He worked for this man three summers already," I explained, hoping to assure Dad that there was a mature, stable college kid involved with the operation. Dad probably knew what I was attempting but he did not bother to investigate my implication that a "mature, stable" college kid might be involved.

"How would you get to Oklahoma and how would you get back home if you did this?" was Dad's next question.

"Mark said I could fly down there and then fly back," I reported.

"That is going to cut into your money," Dad observed.

"I guess so but I could still make some money," was all I could muster. It was an issue I had not rehearsed. Until now the interrogation had been going well.

"So you wouldn't need to be driven down there?" he wanted to know.

"I don't think you would have to," I answered.

He seemed done with his concerns but then continued with, "Is anyone else from your school going?"

"I don't know Dad," I said. "There might be lots of kids who saw the ad."

Mom was in the room and listening but I could not see her reactions to all of this. Dad was silent for a minute. I was silent too and acting nonchalant. The acting was not good but the heart was there.

Dad looked at Mom and without any nod or even a raised eyebrow got what must have been an affirmative nod.

"All right, Dave, I guess you can do this," was the verdict.

"Thank you Dad!" I said, trying to be clearly appreciative without being too excited. "Thank you Mom."

Dad smiled a sly little, "You really sweated through that one!" kind of a smile. Mom said, "Just be careful," and walked out of the living room. She was OK with me going but her motherly anxiety was clearly rising as she agreed to let the first child fly from the nest, if even for a summer. Her issue may have been more the destination of the flight than the flight itself.

I retreated to my room and savored the front edge of my adventure. My siblings did not yet know that I had permission for a whole summer away, that I had pulled off the request of a lifetime. The baby had lived the night and I would now nurture it to maturity out of the eye-shot of my parents and out of the earshot of my siblings. I was not going to expose this precious adventure to any possible harm due to my own carelessness. The next time I raised the idea the baby was going to be robust and thriving.

After supper, I used the phone in my folk's room and called Mark Wheeler to tell him I wanted the job. After working out some details, he also volunteered that another student had signed up: another junior named Dan Tennyson. I had no idea who he was. As a first-year transfer student I only knew 30 or 40 of the 800 juniors at Central High.

Dan would prove to be a gear-stripping friend for me; pushing me far beyond my comfort zone. I had always worked hard to align my life with kids like me: comfortable kids, predictable kids, safe kids, sports kids. Dan was none of these. The ultimate victory of my summer may have been that I came to care about Dan despite the oceanic differences between a tightly wound jock and a mostly unwound pothead.

I called Dan that night, and we ate lunch together the next day. We were two very different boys on the exterior with one very identical streak on the interior: we were both risk-takers at one level or another. We were both hooked by "travel required." My bent for risk and pioneering was more subtle and late blooming than Dan's. In the last two days my bent for these had taken a big step.

Since that day in the Central High lunchroom, I have met 40 men like Dan, but he was my first encounter with this breed. He was cocky but not fully arrogant. He was a long haired, foul mouthed, big talking, drug using, jittery bundle of likeability and insecurity. I did not see it at the time but most of Dan's energy and wild proclamations came from his screaming inner uncertainty about who he was and what people really felt about him. Dan had no gates or filters on his words and therefore said whatever came into his mind—relationally kosher or not. Some of these crazy declarations arose from Dan's considerable intellect and his love of "shock value."

On our first lunch meeting Dan declared, "You and I are going to be great friends!"

Later that summer, on a clear, warm afternoon driving a wheat truck down the highway Dan suddenly proclaimed, "I feel horrible! I'm sick! I'm having hallucinations and everything!"

At the very beginning of our summer together, on a drive to an amusement park with me and two girls he had never met he said, "I need to find a place to drop a load!" He was referring to drugs, but we were thinking other things.

Dan both entertained himself and evaluated his own worth by meticulously studying the various reactions to his outlandish proclamations. All the while he pretended not to notice in the slightest what someone thought or did in response. Believing he had no place in the world, Dan set out to change his own mind by acting as if he had the only place in the world.

Our first three weeks together must have been heaven for Dan. Here was a stiff, naive, quiet, straight-laced, toe-the-line, what-are-others-thinking-about-me, stay-out-of-trouble, do-the-right-thing, church youth group president. He had things to say about everything that I had never heard before. He had a philosophy of life that I had never heard, nor could I dream up in a decade of sleepless concentration. I was the summer-long victim of Dan's emanating anxiety and self-doubt. He needed someone to vibrate, and I was ripe for the agitation. As the summer went on and I was less agitated by his insanity he eased up and pulled more inside himself. It is a wonder that I remember him so fondly.

Once I met Dan it seemed that I saw him all over the place. I half feared that he would drop out of the trip and half hoped he would. The longer I knew Dan in that spring semester the more I became convinced that he would drop out. Before the trip Dan changed or missed almost everything that he had committed to do. I felt sure he would not go.

I was going and I was preparing like a boy scout before a winter camp out. With the guidance of my Dad I bought a green Army surplus duffel bag for my gear. A combination lock for the top of my duffel bag was my next purchase. I carefully and dutifully memorized the combination. The boots and gloves were all new and squeaky clean and shouting, "This kid is new to farm work." I wrote my name in the clothes and shoes and my name with full address in huge letters on the duffel bag:

Dave Gibson
PO Box 40
Nemo, South Dakota

All this meticulous preparation and precaution with my gear would seem fully ludicrous when the summer was over. That duffel bag would be out of my watchful care most of the time. It would be in the back of a dozen pickups, under the bunk in uncounted trailer parks, under my cot in two different barns and under the trailer house in rain storms. It could have been cut open by the pocket knife of any one of thirty crew members and vagrants who wandered in and out of its presence over the next 90 days.

That the bag came home with its contents, without a slit, and with the lock still attached is minor miracle. One of my gifts in life has been to prepare incessantly for adventures that turn out to be ragged-edge rodeos for which no one could have prepared. When I get home from these sorted forays, tattered but intact, I was grateful to have survived and amused at what I thought I was doing to prepare against every eventuality.

This sudden burst of responsibility still did not slop over into my studies, but I was keeping my grades high enough to keep out of summer school, to advance to twelfth grade, and to not jeopardize my looming adventure.

At 16 everything was intense and difficult and important and anxious and consuming; how I did in sports, how bad I did in school, how the red-headed girl treated me, how I got along with everyone, how I looked to others. It was the stage of life when desire is intense, insecurity is substantial, and wisdom is scarce or altogether absent.

Unlike many teens I contained the various meltdowns in my life inside of myself. I didn't have great trouble getting along with others—I had great trouble getting along with myself. My anxieties, intensities and foolishness were mostly shielded in my relationships by my intense desire to be liked and my great acting ability; however inside I had a racing mind, an anxious heart, and a gift for always seeing the worst case scenario. Obsessing on existing problems or potential troubles was the air I breathed. As a bonus, I had no mediating voice inside of myself or outside of myself to say, "Calm down and be rational for a minute."

Now that I had the job, I would join the crew in Fort Sill, Oklahoma as soon as school was out. I would need a plane ticket to Oklahoma City and a bus ticket to Fort Sill. I had traveled all over the West, but it was all in the back seat of my father's tired string of Ford station wagons. I had never seen the inside of an airplane and never even been to a bus station.

My folks bought me a plane ticket from Rapid City to Denver to Oklahoma City and a bus ticket to Lawton, Oklahoma. Dan was to be on my same flights and same bus. We had an overnight stay in Denver. My parents arranged for us to stay with neighbors from where we had lived only ten months earlier. Our adventure did not wait for Fort Sill— it launched in Denver.

2 THE LAUNCH

I have often experienced a strange, difficult dance between,
"I can't wait!" and "I don't want to go!"
Truth is I couldn't wait.
When the time came, I did go.

The spring semester ended quickly and my junior year, like my previous school years, was mediocre but over. I had suffered through my standard pathetic track season; with great effort I threw the discus a few feet farther than our trainer. I had admired a red-haired girl, from a distance, and vowed that in my senior year I would actually talk to her. I had collected my usual slate of B's and C's. I had cleaned out my locker and said my goodbyes.

I met my ever-popular younger brother at Dad's Bronco and drove the familiar winding, forest-lined miles to Boxelder Job Corps Center. Alan and I mostly drove in silence. Neither one of us were very good at relationships or even at small talk. Our lives were already diverging. I felt helpless to reach across the widening gap.

The too familiar mixture of relief and regret was swirling inside me. I was relieved that another year was over and I had passed. But I regretted that once again I had not applied myself. I had friends who took books home and actually studied, ran extra miles for fitness during sports seasons, and kept their stuff organized. I envied them and yet had resigned to never enjoy diligence in my own life. It was a major act of discipline for me to brush my teeth before bed. I hated this about myself but neither understood it nor could fix it. This year I would have less time than normal for these regrets.

The day after school ended, my parents drove me into Rapid City and then beyond to the airport east of town. Dan and I would be flying together to Oklahoma. We could not fly from Rapid City to Oklahoma City in one day—neither Rapid City nor Oklahoma City were hubs of anything. Our first flight was to Denver where we planned to stay overnight with friends of mine. Only a year earlier my dad had been transferred from Denver on his latest job ricochet around the Mountain West.

Inside the terminal I immediately took care of my duffel bag and ticket. Dan was already there with his parents. They were sitting in the shiny, molded plastic chairs and joking with each other. Dan had not checked in, nor was he anxious to do so. I was instantly anxious about Dan meeting my folks and about all he might say or do.

"You ready to go, weenie?" asked Dan. I mumbled an embarrassed, "I guess so." We were little more than strangers, yet Dan felt full freedom to assume the familiarity of ten-year friends.

"This is my folks and my 'sinister' and my worthless brothers," was his introduction of his family. "I'm Dave Gibson and this is my mom and dad," I replied.

Our parents shook hands and the gulf between their vulgar easiness and my family's responsible stiffness made for an immediate silence. There was nowhere to go with a conversation.

In Dan's family belittling each other was an art form. They cussed. They joked. They made obscene gestures as a matter of routine interaction. The family seemed to suffer from a collective, genetic mania that made stillness impossible, quietness unthinkable and civil conversation foreign. They made me beyond uneasy—especially in the presence of my parents.

We Gibsons were straight-laced people. Obscenities, coming from the mouth or the hand, were unimaginable in the presence of our family. We not only did not act like Dan and his family, but we also took a Pharisaical stance toward them.

The meeting between our two contrasting families was complicated by my utter absence of personal boundaries. I had zero concept of what was my responsibility and what was not. If Dan and his family or anyone else offended my parents I felt it would be my fault. I approached all of life as a person who was responsible for everything bad that I did and also for everything bad that happened in my general vicinity. The final result is that I carried guilt for a load of things over which I had no control. Strange as it seems I felt somehow responsible and at severe fault for the behavior of these people whom I had never met and over whom I had no control.

In reaction to this uneasy drama, Dad gave a lame excuse about wanting to go over some last minute details with me and the three of us moved off to the far wall—but not far enough to be out of earshot. As we walked away, they resumed their manic ridicule of each other.

From across the waiting area the three of us tried to concentrate on our conversation while casting sideward glances at their ongoing family circus. I was afraid that my parents already regretted letting me take the job.

"I would keep your duffel bag locked whenever you are not with it," my dad instructed again. "And keep your gear together. Folks on crews like this have a habit of walking off with things. Guys on our fire crews will take about anything and I am sure this is no different."

"I will," I assured him with every intention of watching my stuff diligently. What I did not know is that no wheatie, no matter how destitute or ill-willed, really had much interest in my worn and smelly socks.

"Let us know how you are and where you are," my mother instructed.

"I will, Mom," I said with the best intentions.

"I wish we knew how to get a hold of you," she worried.

"I can call now and then," was the best I could offer, but it didn't sound reassuring.

More folks arrived for our flight and Dan finally checked in. Across the room his family continued their antics, and everyone in the growing crowd was aware of their family comedy. For this family, life was theater.

Dan was not a high school thespian who lived for drama class. Wherever he found himself became the set. Dan was the lead. Any person near Dan was a player who existed as a convenient straight man, useful only to make Dan look clever, funny, and intelligent.

In retrospect Dan was probably the most insecure person I had met. He was incessantly acting, talking, jesting and sling-shooting himself into the center of the available attention. He had a rare gift for shocking statements and all of them asking, "Does anyone notice me?" "Does anyone care about me?" "Do I matter to anyone?" "Am I worth anything?" These questions all remained unanswered, driving Dan to his incessant demand for the limelight. Seeing the dynamics of his family made it clear where his insecurity was bred. Just as I could not see my miserable lack of boundaries, Dan could not see that he had internalized the family put-downs.

Bravado was his prescription for the pain and put-downs his prescription for insecurity. He had used bravado so long that he was deep into the phase of diminishing returns.

I was greatly relieved when the flight was announced, bringing an end to this uneasy situation. Dan and his family were hugging and jesting, me and my family shaking hands and exchanging last minute cautions. The parting for the three of us was awkward.

Besides almost always feeling awkward around my parents, I did not trust airplanes. The one previous flight in my life had been in a small plane over Yellowstone Park. The rough air had terrorized me as I spent two hours knowing without any doubt that I would die. I rode in the back of that small plane behind my dad and the pilot with my fingers dug into the bottom of my seat praying continually and earnestly. Every updraft and every downdraft sent my heart rate higher and my finger nails deeper into the cushions.

I was in internal terror now but too self-conscious to act out the terror. I got on the metal bird with the quiet determination of a man who was going to be hanged for his crimes and who intended to go out with dignity. A lesser man would scream, kick, fight, bite, and exhaust every ounce of energy to save himself at this last minute. I would not go out that way. Despite my life of crime, at least my grieving mother could say that I had died in the manner of a gentleman.

The flight was uneventful. I was neither hanged nor killed in a crash. There were no downdrafts, no updrafts and no fingers dug into the seat, though the prayer persisted. I expended ample emotional energy internalizing my terror. It was an Oscar-winning performance, and I was both the actor and the audience. Between Dan and I, I was the better actor, though neither he nor any other soul knew.

The visit to Denver would be the first of many surreal experiences in those ninety days of adventure. I landed in a place that had been my home just ten months earlier and found that it was all strange and distant—visually almost the same, but experientially faded, emotionally disconnected, and plastered over with forgetting and with not belonging. I never have understood this strange feeling. I saw the places and knew in my mind that they were the same. But in my heart I felt that I had only dreamed them. Mostly I knew that I did not belong here anymore. That sadness was heightened by knowing that I did not feel I belonged in my new place either. I felt these feelings often since at the age of 16, Denver was the seventh of eight towns where I had lived.

Our former neighbors Carl and Joanne Field met us at the airport. Carl was exactly like I had remembered him but Joanne was much heavier in just the few months since I had moved. Something felt awkward about being with them. This was strange to me because we had enjoyed a generally easy relationship before. Years later I learned that these two were at that time only months from divorce. Whatever had gone wrong in their relationship was now making it awkward for them to be with me.

"Wow, you're even taller than last year, kid!" was Carl's greeting. "Have you been eating your peas?"

"I guess so," I said with a grin.

In my own insecurity I always loved affirmations for being tall. I had been growing and was now 6'3". I had not eaten more than my share of peas, but apparently the modest amount of peas that I had eaten had been especially good to me.

The Fields took us to their home on Carr Street which was directly across from our old house at 1601 S. Carr. In just one year both our old houses had gotten smaller.

Carl and Joanne's house now sat on what had been a vacant lot when our family moved onto Carr Street. That vacant lot was half of our go-cart track. The track was a figure-eight with sharp, banked turns and weed infields and crude jumps. My brother and I had bought a used go-cart for $18—cleaning out all our silver dollars, regular dollars, and all our change. We kept the cart running all summer with frequent repairs of wire and tape and tinkering. At the end of that dirt track summer my dad had taken the motor to a small engine shop where it was pronounced dead on arrival. Along with breathing the thin mountain air the poor beast had breathed too much dust and scoured out her lone cylinder beyond repair.

Our beloved machine was dead for good but we would both remember that summer with the "good old days" kind of fondness that ferments to a wonderful sweetness over the decades. Ferments until you forget the fights over who was going to ride next and the muffler burns and the dirt sprayed in your face and the scrapes and the hours of coaxing her to start and the frustrating days when she would not run at all.

Decades out all we remember is the pleasure of speed and the banked turn and the sound of power and the envy of kids who were not allowed to ride. We remember the feeling that we were in control and that we were fast and that we were powerful and that we were somebody.

Only months after the death of our go-cart the contractor had broken ground to build the Field's home. It was almost the last home in the neighborhood and the track, along with the cart, became a memory. The Fields planted a lawn, built flower beds where our favorite turn had been, and obliterated forever the beloved trenches where our cobbled machine had carried us on those joy-filled summer laps. On this night I would be sleeping on the very spot where our ragged and dying cart had churned through the dirt and spit rooster tails of dust into the summer dusk of our mile-high home.

My return to this physical place and to these changed people left me unable to assess it all. It was another in a long chain of "returns to former places" in my life as a nomad that heightened the uncertainty about where I belonged and to whom I belonged.

When I knew that Dan and I would be staying over in Denver, I had called a girl I knew from my family's church in Denver named Carrie James. She seemed very happy to hear from me and offered to take Dan and me to Elitch Amusement Park.

When we got to the Fields' home, dinner was ready for us and we ate quickly before Carrie and her friend arrived. I had no sense of the poor etiquette of dropping off my gear, "woofing" down supper and running out for the evening. The Fields understood that I had no sense of etiquette and they understood my interest in Carrie. Carl was almost giddy with the prospect of me having a date of sorts with her.

Carrie and I had been in the same church youth group for two years, and I had been in love with her for the whole time. She was a year older than me and beautiful and kind and smart and very out of my league. She was also very attached to a jock of some fame from another high school. Carrie had some fondness for me, probably like an older sister loves her gangly younger brother who is now taller than her and one tenth as socially savvy. Carrie's boyfriend sensed her fondness for me and went out of his way to treat me with disdain. I tolerated it because I couldn't stop him and because it was worth the abuse to be around Carrie.

Carrie and her friend Janet came for us in a ragged sedan. When Carrie got out of the car she was prettier than my memory had been able to retain. She was still very slight and her face was still Carrie with so many features that I had forgotten. Her face was a unique combination of pretty and angular. She was still the dream girl that she had been, but she was somehow sadder. I was too young and too inept to investigate her sadness.

"You are taller and more handsome than you were," she said as she hugged me.

"Thanks," was my lame reply and already my mind was evaluating that greeting. It was a reply that I would lay awake and correct most of the night.

I was excited, confused and afraid. It was the kind of thing she might say to her kid brother but it didn't feel like kid brother stuff. Something had changed in the very few months that I had been gone.

The shallow introductions made the predictable rounds though our awkward little group. I was connected to the Fields and to Dan and to Carrie and Carrie was connected to Janet. But the Fields did not know Dan or Carrie or Janet; Dan did not know anyone but me; Carrie knew me and Janet but not Dan and the Fields; Janet knew only Carrie. It was one of those bizarre groups that stood on a driveway together for all of two minutes and would never be close to being together again—not even close to being in the same town again even if the town was a big as Denver.

We were barely in the car when Carrie said to me that she was no longer dating the jock or anyone at all. This was fully beyond my belief. Just months ago they had been very close and it was beyond anything I could fathom that a guy would let Carrie get away. She was too beautiful, too unique, too amazing, too special—outwardly so attractive but inwardly even more beautiful. I asked her what had happened and she would only say, "We just moved on from each other." The sentence felt very painful. It also felt like a lie.

Carrie and I sat in the back seat—heart pounding stuff for me. Janet drove. Dan sat in the front passenger seat and began to stake out center stage for himself. His personal drama was quickly in high gear. It was like opening night with a brand new audience, and there were girls in the audience to boot. Dan's theatrics filled the old car and spilled out the open windows. The girls, new to Dan's presence, tested the situation trying to decide whether to laugh or run for their lives. Even with the windows open Dan was using most of the oxygen.

Both Carrie and Janet were instantly uneasy. My general anxiety around Dan rose another level. As Dan spoke and joked and gestured I could see Janet glancing in the rearview mirror at Carrie and Carrie looking back. They were working to communicate with each with only glances in a mirror. They were probably successful but as a teenage male I had no idea what they were saying to each other. At one moment I thought they might laugh. Time after time I thought they would laugh at the insanity of Dan's instant bravado. Somehow they never did. If I had possessed any sense of propriety I would have said, "Dan, these girls don't even know you. Ratchet down a bit." Instead I just ratcheted up my own anxiety.

We were scarcely out of the neighborhood when Dan announced, "I need to find someplace to drop a load."

What sounded like a severe need to have a bowel movement was actually a severe desire to "drop a load" of drugs down his throat. Dan had drugs that he had brought from home. He had known Carrie and Janet for literally two minutes and he was announcing this.

My summer partner was a druggie. I'm sure there were clues to this before this night but I had not seen them. I had visions of our being stopped, searched, arrested and sent to the federal penitentiary for a couple of decades.

But my greater anxiety was the fact that for the first time in my life I was sitting in the back seat of a car with a girl.

The scene inside this aging sedan was a case of regular folks in a crazy play. An imaginative playwright would have been hard pressed to dream it up. Dan was acting. Janet was driving and worrying and watching Dan beside her and watching the road in front of her and worrying about Carrie and me in the back seat—stealing glances in the mirror at her best friend and a fresh-faced teenager whom she did not trust.

When we got to Elitch Park, Carrie and I went one way and Dan and Janet went another. We had no plan and no particular goals, at least I did not. Perhaps Carrie did. Carrie and I wandered through the park, talked, looked at stuff and rode a few rides. In addition to being afraid of airplanes, I was afraid of rides and heights and small places. Carrie convinced me to go on a wooden roller coaster that looped out over the lake. Other than sheer terror, I had no good reason not to ride. Just as I would not allow myself to show terror to a plane full of passengers, I could not show terror to Carrie. So, for the third time in one day, I was terrorized and no one knew.

To my surprise and relief I was not killed on the coaster. At a couple of points I even let myself have fun. There remains today a stark black and white photo in my mind, the long curve of the coaster out over the lake. It is dark. The coaster careens out over the blackness of the lake. Carrie and I are clutching the handrail. The coaster car is banking hard to the left. Carrie is forced against me or maybe lets herself drift against me. The lights of Denver are dotted in the distance across the lake—a thin line of white points along the shore. The night stars are barely visible above the dotted lights. The intensity of the instant painted the image forever in my mind as if this is the last thing I would ever see before I was rocketed into the black night and into the black water of Elitch Lake and into the black terror of unconsciousness. The car held to the tracks and I held to the car and we both lived. The feel of Carrie pressed against me has faded. But the mental picture of the black lake and the white lights of the shore of Denver never went away.

As it got late, Elitch got fairly quiet on this warm summer night. The park's crowd had dwindled as kids wandered off to drive or eat or to summer curfews. Carrie and I talked about my life in South Dakota and her life in Denver and walked some more and then we were holding hands. Anxiety and excitement fought inside me. In one of those unreal moments, when the mind both stops and races, and the memory will not faithfully record anything, we stopped in a lonely corner of the park.

As I thought about it later I realized that we both stopped. We turned to each other at the same time and I leaned down to her and she reached up to me. We kissed each other and stood there kissing for a long time. The experience overwhelmed my memory. I know it happened but cannot fully retrieve it. I was a sixteen-year-old socially inept gangly moose of a kid kissing my dream girl.

Carrie was experienced at kissing and I was not. I kissed her way too hard and it hurt her. When she could not take the pain anymore she gently explained this to me. I felt like a boy scout in a military war room, like a little league pitcher on the Red Sox mound. What was I doing here with her—other than demonstrating myself to be a child? I added embarrassment to my emotions.

We stood in the near-deserted park and continued kissing Finally Carrie said, "We better find Dan and Janet."

"We should," I agreed but would have happily stood there until dawn.

Reluctantly we started back to the car to see if Dan and Janet were ready to leave. We were walking slowly and savoring the connection that we had toyed with for two years.

When we came to the parking lot we could see three people attempting to break into Janet's car, over a hundred yards away.In a small sliver of time our mood was jolted from romantic connection to fearful unbelief.

We stopped walking, edged behind a service truck, and began to watch the trio work on the car. They had some kind of a tool and the one of the three was trying to force it into the window. Their backs were to us and even lumped together they were not terribly obvious in the mosaic of shadows and scattered cars in the massive lot. All we could see was the main guy working on the window was a Hispanic man about twenty-five- years-old.

In disbelief we moved quietly back into the park and began running to find a security guard. When we found one, a young beefy man with no pistol and with a great exhilaration that finally something dangerous was happening, we told him that someone was trying to break into our car. He asked where the car was, the description of the bandits and the kind of car. We ran towards the parking lot and the beefy security officer left us at the gate of the park while he lumbered in a rhino-like sprint to confront the thieves. When he approached the group the trio turned and looked at him with curiosity but did not run. The officer stopped right on top of the three and took a menacing stance. Then the four of them simply began to talk. They talked together for less than a minute and we could see one of the three showing the guard what was probably a driver's license. Carrie and I stood in the shadows perplexed.

Soon the guard returned to us and said, "The girl owns the car and she locked her keys inside and one of our maintenance guys is trying to get it open for her."

"OK, well thanks for checking," I said, "We thought they were trying to steal it."

"Better to be safe than sorry," he replied as he walked away. His chest was still heaving from his excited sprint, and I was reeling from my foolish assumption.

We had turned in Janet for trying to get into her own car. We took the long, sheepish walk across the lot to face the three of them. The three men working on the car mercilessly reinforced our feeling of idiocy. The maintenance guy, armed with the highly technical and effective auto theft tool of a straightened-out coat hanger with a loop on the end, eventually got the door unlocked and walked off still smiling. We piled into our stolen car and drove onto the school-is-out-night streets of Denver.

On the ride home Carrie and I continued to make out in the back seat. Dan and Janet tried to talk and not pay attention. Dan was more subdued than usual—perhaps due to the effects of having "dropped a load." Too soon we were back on Carr Street, getting out of the car, saying goodbye, and watching them go. Carrie climbed out of the back seat into the front, waved to me, and then it was over. She left like she had been playing with a toy that she simply knew she could not have anymore.

I stood for a bit on the sidewalk wondering what this meant. Here was a girl with whom I had been madly in love just one year earlier; back then she was not even close to available. Now, after an evening of walking and talking and hand-holding and kissing she had driven off. I would never see her again. It was one of billions of "what the heck was that?" incidents in the boy/girl world. I would wonder about what might have been for a long time. But I mostly wondered why I didn't feel something more for this girl who one year earlier had been my "dream girl."

Years later a mutual friend told me that she married a professional baseball player, had a bunch of kids and may or may not have lived happily ever after. I hope she did. She deserved it. She was very kind to a gangly, naive kid one evening at Elitch's.

The morning after my first kiss, the flight to Oklahoma City was less terror-filled then previous flights. We found our bags at baggage claim and walked to the bus terminal in the airport. Our next leg to meet up with our harvest crew was from Oklahoma City to Lawton via Greyhound. The crew had already been together for a few weeks cutting wheat in southern Oklahoma. The two of us were the last to join the crew and being the new kid would be an anxious thing for me. I should have been good at being the new kid after having been to two elementary schools, two junior highs, and two high schools. It didn't seem to get easier.

I placed my duffle bag carefully in the belly of the bus. I found a bin that seemed empty and put my bag against the wall, calculating where it might be out of all harm's way. Dan pitched his bag into the bin closest to the door and climbed aboard. Mr. Carefree and Mr. Cautious were beginning their summer together.

The bus was crammed. Dan and I ended up in an aisle full of people standing shoulder to shoulder holding the shiny, greasy hand rails and knocking into each other like beads on a wire each time the bus stopped or started. As we jerked out of the terminal and down the airport drive I could see nothing except the bags and packages in the overhead bins above the seated riders. The only way to see out was to crouch down and peer through the window at the passing Oklahoma flat-scape.

I crouched down at the entrance of the airport to see several huge fountains of water bubbling up on both sides of the road. They looked like they had a pump with huge capacity and power. A surprising amount of water was shooting twenty feet into the air. It seemed odd to create these great fountains at the entrance to an airport where water did not seem abundant and the fountains did not seem to fit. I asked someone in the seat next to me if they were fountains and was amazed to hear the explanation of the working of an artesian well. I was amazed like the country boy who fell off of his dad's turnip truck. This was another serving in what would be a long summer of education doled out in pieces almost every day—and some days in very big pieces.

Not being able to see what was going by outside was discouraging no matter how boring the scenes might have been. I loved watching country go by—any kind of country. I had watched uncountable and unmemorable mountains, forests, lakes, snow drifts, farms, towns, and valleys go by the windows of my dad's cars. It didn't bore me. Standing in the bus aisle I had a still-life view of someone's overnight case and Piggly Wiggly sack. The unenjoyable ride was minor but one of the first in a long string of disappointments. When something negative and unexpected happened my father would usually say, "That's a revolting development." The summer would be a long parade of them for me.

Despite having never driven a combine, never driven a wheat truck, never been on a harvest crew and never even been in a field where a harvest was happening, I had planned out the summer in my head. I had decided how it should go. Where I got the data for how things would be is shrouded in mystery. But I was a boy with expectations about all things future. This summer was to be an incessant string of departures from my pre-scripted plan. As with most of my life, I am sure the summer was richer for the changes from my script, and I was richer for the troubles and disappointments. On that day I did not understand that looking at a Piggly Wiggly bag instead at a farm house was inconsequential, so negligible that it should not be remembered.

As the trip wore on people began to leave the bus in one little burg after another, but no one seemed to be getting on. Eventually enough people had left that all of us standing in the aisle got a place to sit and I began to stare out the window—past an old, sad woman—as the sights of southern Oklahoma lumbered past my bus window. Inside our Greyhound the heat was stifling even with every window open. It could get hot in the various mountain towns where I had lived, but nothing like this. Sweat ran down my temples and down the small of my back. My wet shirt stuck to the plastic seat. The hot air blasting in on me sucked out the moisture that had not been sweated out of me.

Outside in the heat of southern Oklahoma, stationed at varied distances along the highway, stood tired towns and tired farms and tired people. I loved watching them.

Save for two years in Presidio, Texas as a toddler—years I could not remember—I had never lived in the South or even been in the South. I had never read about the South. The closest I could come to anything "South" was seeing "Gone with the Wind" with Carrie when she was "taken" and I was thinking about her more than Rhett Butler "not giving a damn."

This was all new to me—authentic culture shock for a northern kid. There were literally more African Americans on one bus that I had seen in my entire northern upbringing, drawled words and sentences I could not decipher, expressions I did not understand, clothing I had not seen, stores I had never heard of, and license plates I did not know.

The culture shock, the heat, the being away from home, the uneasiness about Dan, the confusion about Carrie, and the uncertainties about the crew and the boss and the work all piled on and made me a little numb. I was in one of my "keep going though this doesn't feel too good and try not to think about it too much" modes of life.

We arrived in Lawton about the middle of the afternoon, pulled our bags from the belly of the bus and began walking to a trailer park. Our new employer had given us the name of a trailer park where his trailers were stationed for the duration of the stay in Lawton. We asked directions several times and walked a long way in the heat of the Okie afternoon. My duffle was stuffed with too much "just in case" stuff, causing the strap to bite into my shoulder. Dan walked with his carefree "this should be interesting" stance and I beside him with my vigilant "we need to find this place" anxiety.

In an hour or a little more, with sweat dripping from us, we arrived at what was easily the dreariest and dumpiest trailer park I had ever seen. I had lived in trailer parks more than once in my vagabond life and some of them plenty ragged—but none this tattered. Some of the trailers were the homes of permanent residents and some were the shoddily, hastily hooked-up trailers of wheat crews. The place was fairly quiet with the wheaties gone to the fields. We found someone at home who knew Don's trailers and showed us which one was the crew trailer. He said that the crew would not be home for hours.

A nicer trailer, our stained t-shirted guide told us, was the summer home of Don and his wife and their three children. They were not home either.

Still gripping my bag, I stepped inside the crew trailer and looked at what my mother would call a pig sty.

The place was filthy. It was not just dirty. It was not just cluttered. It stunk. The smell was assaulting. The trailer house had been converted from a one bedroom to an "all bedroom" bunk house. The entire length was bunk beds made from two-by-fours and plywood and ratty mattresses. They were the kind of mattresses that you laugh at as they lie in the ditch next to a road and jokingly say, "Hey, there is a good looking piece of furniture! Want to stop and pick it up?" They were the kind with stains and stuffing and odors coming out, the kind that make prime real estate for mice or worse.

This trailer was in its fifth or sixth year as a crew trailer and had not been cleaned, ever. It might be that Don or his wife went into it at the beginning of the summer and threw out the left-behind clothes and soap bars and pornographic magazines from the past summer. But it was not cleaned. The result was a long, narrow, grungy metal rectangle that housed dirty men and that grew more and more dirty with time.

I set my bag gingerly on the floor next to the door and investigated the rest of the trailer. The shower was the most severely disgusting place in the trailer, and I decided that I could make it through an entire summer without a shower. I committed to myself that I could go the whole summer caked in dried sweat, wheat chaff in every crack I owned, sweat-salt lining my face, body odor reeking, fingernails grimy, and hands black with filth and never set foot on the slimy, fungus covered, germ infested floor of that miniature shower. That vow was broken the very next day.

I went deeper into culture shock. In the decades to follow I would experience culture shock of one degree or another in thirty or more countries. Those decades later I would know what it was. On that hot summer afternoon I had no idea what was happening to me but I knew I didn't want to be here.

Since the crew was gone Dan and I left our gear on the floor of the trailer and walked back out into the streets of Lawton. Now there was nothing for us to do but wander. In that afternoon, before I was a reader and a writer and before I absolutely lusted for discretionary time, I was bitterly bored and Dan was worse than me. We walked, talked and made up not-very-funny jokes. We ridiculed people we did not know. We belittled buildings and stores we did not understand. We tried to find some equilibrium in the spinning new world we had entered and sought that equilibrium mostly in ridicule for this new world.

We returned to the crew trailer twice but still no one was home. We walked more—moving slowly past aging homes, tired stores and heat-humbled people. The heat held everyone in slow motion. The town felt exhausted but determined with its faded paint, sagging fences, un-mowed, heat-withered grass, gigantic weeds, cracked driveways, sleeping dogs, and sloping porches. Elderly black men sat in the shade of old trees on nylon woven lawn chairs with a drink, a smile and no discernible thing to do. Sprinklers left far too long in one spot turned the ground within their reach into a mud fields under the heat scorched grass and weeds. Cars with a corner up on cinder blocks revealed various brake parts in shoe boxes underneath. Weeds grew up through a bike that had not been moved since spring.

Lawton wore her fatigue like so many towns where people are striving and surviving but not close to thriving. At the beginning of their day they tackle the work with a new determination and at the end of the day they come home exhausted and beaten down in spirit. They sit on the porch in front of a fan, drink a few cold beers and talk with their neighbors and families. They don't finish the brake job they started and don't mow the lawn and don't paint the trim and don't pick up the bike. Late at night, they shuffle to bed carrying the fan from the porch, lay on sweaty sheets while the fan blows on them, and listen to the cicadas while fighting to sleep despite their fatigue.

After hours of walking through this faded town and long after dark Dan and I wandered back to the park. Still no one. Finally, at about eleven at night we put our sleeping bags on the lawn in front of the trailer and tried to sleep. We had only been lying down for ten minutes when the headlights of two pickups and a hot Camaro turned into the park. We jumped up, feeling foolish for planning to sleep on the dirt.

The ragged crew poured slowly from the trucks. It was clear that all but the three drivers had been in some stage of sleep.

A grimy man of maybe 38 walked toward us from the first pickup. He carried a big beer belly that slopped over his belt generously. He stood maybe five foot nine inches. His hair resembled a shock of wheat that had been hit by a dust devil. Chewing tobacco ran down the crack at the corner of his mouth on his chubby face. As he got closer I could read "Dexter Custom Harvesting" above the pocket of a sweat-stained shirt. The man was not unfriendly, but he had no use for small talk and relationship building—especially in his exhausted state.

Don Dexter came up to us and shook our hands. His handshake was anemic, limp, and creepy. It felt like a man "handing you a dead fish" as my father would say.

Don showed Dan to the only bunk that was not spoken for and told me that I had no bunk and would need to set up an army cot wherever we landed. I was relieved. Then he said that for tonight I should climb in the bunk of one of the guys who had gone home for a couple of days. I became depressed. I would rather have slept on the ground but determined to sleep on my sleeping bag and touch nothing of the "linens" on the bunk of this unknown wheatie.

After Don had walked off toward his trailer Mark Wheeler introduced himself. Mark was the college student who had recruited Dan and me, and was one of the pickup drivers. Mark came over to welcome us in his aloof, disinterested way. He was the supervisor of the crew in that he worried about the wheaties and the machinery while Don worried about the wheat and the money. This was Mark's fourth summer with Don Dexter Custom Harvesting and he clearly knew the ropes. The crew did not respect him much because of his thinly veiled arrogance and because he was a college boy. Mark had little use for high school kids who wrecked trucks or for anyone who did not work hard or for thirty-ish drifters who did not possess the personal responsibility of a riverboat gambler.

Ramrodding this harvest crew was a stepping stone for Mark. It was the last "low" thing that he planned to do before he earned an engineering degree and began drawing a real salary with full benefits, lived in one town, bought a house, invested in a tax-deferred annuity, became respectable, stable, and middle class and slept in clean sheets in a room that did not reek. Mark knew his job and he did not care what the others thought of him. He knew he needed the job and he also knew that he did not need to take it much longer.

The full crew consisted of nine guys plus Don and his wife. The other guys gave Dan and I their names or not and most did not offer their hands as they shuffled into the trailer—some to the shower and some to bed.

The trailer where I was to spend my summer, I was soon to learn, housed no adults. Some of the residents were nearly as old as my parents but they were not, by any sane definition, adults. The residents of this aluminum box were mostly ragged, mostly poor owing to bad choices, mostly immature, and largely lazy. Most were thoroughly self-absorbed, generally addicted in various ways, reliably dishonest, and famously apathetic about cleanliness, courtesy and order.

A couple of the other crew members beside Dan and I were high school kids. What mattered to these boys was beer, finishing the summer as quickly as possible, and college money—in that order. One of the boys was from Don's hometown and did not want to be here. I learned later that the boy's father had secured this job with Don without the boy knowing. He spent most of the entire summer being sullen and distant. The other boy was kind, tall, and very powerful. He proved to be friendly when he wanted to be. However, he was a severe introvert and much preferred to be quietly alone.

More than half the men on Don's crew were in their mid-thirties to mid-forties, divorced, usually unemployed, ragged, untrustworthy, heavy drinkers and chain smokers. What mattered to these boys was money, fresh cigarettes, avoiding hard work, getting laid without getting involved, cold beer and crude jokes. The trail behind them was two to three decades long—hard living and hard results—scattered with the jetsam of their foolishness and the flotsam of their bondages.

To my great delight these ragged older drifters left me alone. I never understood why. It may have been that Don Dexter made it clear to them that any fighting or stealing or personal animosity was to be directed toward other crews. It may be that they weren't sure they wanted to tackle with a six-foot three-inch high school football player. It may be that they took me as so green, naïve and boyish that any taking advantage of me would be unethical even in their "code of conduct." If I were to bet today, I would bet on the latter.

Three older guys on the crew had known each other since grade school in their hometown somewhere in Oklahoma. They had been bouncing around together for years. It seemed amazing that they stayed together given their general self-absorption and incessant bent for taking advantage of others. Perhaps they had some unspoken pact to not take advantage of each other. These three enjoyed a twisted synergy that kept them apparently happy and relatively satisfied.

All three were heavy drinkers, heavy womanizers when a desperate woman could be found and all three poster boys for irresponsibility—possessing the ambition of a railroad tie. Two of the three were incurably tricky—opportunistic for any chance to take advantage of a misplaced pack of cigarettes or an unwatched wallet. One of the three had managed, by some twist of luck, to save enough money to buy, or maybe he had stolen, a red Chevy Camaro. The car was his pride and joy and the three of them piled into it and headed for town any time there was the slightest break in the work—which usually meant sometime between ten o'clock and midnight. They were the only ones who had a car with them for the summer and it was their ticket to the bars, the women, and the gambling that they apparently needed to keep going.

The three were slaves to their own appetites and the cost of that slavery was evident even to the untrained eye. The most striking evidence came every morning when Don rolled us out of bed.

When that call came, the three musketeers would stagger from their bunks reeking of sweat, smoke, and stale beer, stumble out the trailer door on teetering legs, light up a smoke before their eyes adjusted to the daylight and shuffle to the Dexter's trailer without a single grunt to acknowledge "Good morning," or "I see you there," or "I'm ready," or even, "I know I look like death propped up."

By the time they got to the field, they were awake and would climb onto their respective combines and keep them in line and turn right when needed. To keep the combine in line all day and play hard most of the night for most of the summer was quite a feat. Still, I think I learned something during almost ninety mornings of watching that trio labor from their bunk beds to the Dexter's trailer for breakfast and then on to the field.

The eight of us under Mark were evenly and permanently divided into two crews: four combine drivers and four truck drivers. I was a truck driver. How Don decided who was going to drive what rig I do not know. While I was disappointed at first to hear that I would drive a truck, it turned out that I was glad to have drawn a truck.

I was disappointed about not driving combine because I wanted to drive that big, loud, powerful, wheat-eating machine. It seemed that the person piloting that monster, high in the air and making the machine go and stop and turn with ease, was a powerful man. What I did not know, but what I learned a little during the summer, is that I do not like incessantly repetitive things. Driving the wheat inhaling behemoth for eight to sixteen hours a day, and making a right turn about every eight to sixteen minutes, was about as incessantly repetitive as things come.

As it turned out I would drive a combine on the lunch break for one driver or another so he could eat his cold chicken and potato salad in the shade of a pickup. He would sit on the stubble, drink his ice tea, and have a little break from the dust and noise and incessant jarring. He would sit with his head leaning on the shaded door of the pickup, eyes closed, dozing and eating. When he had finished his lunch, I was all too happy to climb down and let him be powerful and dirty and vibrate his teeth and kidneys for the rest of that day.

But tonight, on my first night with the crew and having never set foot in a wheat field, I climbed into the bottom bunk on top of the blankets. I put one of my own T-shirts over the stained pillow in my borrowed bunk. I was tired, but also anxious as usual. I was lying in a short, smelly, borrowed bed and could not sleep for a long, long time. One of the many maladies of anxious people is the inability to sleep. For most of my growing up years I had lain awake for hours on end listening to my younger brother snore and envying his rest. This first night I listened as man after man flopped into his bunk and drifted off into sleep—and some into snoring.

I laid there and listened to sleeping men whom I did not know and looked at the pale light coming through the trailer window and thought. My mind, always working and unwilling to rest, scrolled back through the two days of terror and change and disappointment. I remembered Dan's family and the plane and the roller coaster and Carrie. I remembered the artesian wells and the standing in the aisle. I remembered the hot streets of Lawton and the fact that I had not called my folks to tell them I had arrived.

But mostly I fretted about the dirty bed and about what this summer was going to be like. In my classic anxious fashion, I began enduring the summer. I began checking off the days before the second day was done. I began calculating how much was past and how much was ahead. And just to get an early start on emotional misery, I began feeling homesick. Somewhere in the exhaustion of the day, the heat of the trailer, the snoring in the dark and the emotional ruminations, I fell asleep.

What I could not know that night was that the most difficult days were past me—the first two days. The travel and the stark unknown would soon give way to the next location and the known. I had at least seen the trailer and the crew. I had at least met Don. I had at least gotten to the place. There was plenty more change coming but now I could begin to adjust to what was. Now I could begin to shift to living in my reality—at least my next ninety-day reality. To me at sixteen those ninety days looked very long indeed. They were not. In truth, no stretch of ninety days is very long.

In the morning my education would begin in earnest—my education about the wheaties on our crew; and about the strain and sad distance between Don and Marie; and about heat, dust, and chaff; and about custom wheat harvesting.

My values and way of life were in for a sudden and sharp challenge.

3 LAWTON, OKLAHOMA

When you wake up in a new world,
you'd best get up and tackle it.

I opened my eyes in a new world. I was looking at the bottom of a plywood bunk covered with wheatie "wisdom" recorded with magic markers. It was less compelling than wisdom on a cereal box.

This first morning in Lawton the sun was making an angled shaft of squareness in the dust-filled trailer air. I got up immediately and saw that most of the other bunks were still filled. With a quietness that went beyond courtesy, I pulled on my clothes from the day before. I eased into the closet-like bathroom to relieve myself and stared again in disbelief at the filthiness of that little room. Then I eased out the ill-fitting aluminum door into the Oklahoma morning.

I was apprehensive but for now happy to be in this new world and feeling a little of the elation that "travel required" had stirred in me. My "real" life in South Dakota, though only three days behind me, felt surreal.

One night earlier I had slept in a borrowed bedroom which offered some familiarity in that it sat squarely above my personal go-cart track in a Denver suburb. Outside the window of that bedroom were the tract homes of southwest Denver—including the one I had lived in.

The night before that I had slept in my own bed in the garage that had been remodeled into a bedroom in my parent's home on the Boxelder Job Corps Center. Outside that window the park-like pine forest began immediately. Behind my bedroom the ground climbed steeply toward the top of the mountain. To the side of my bedroom, the ground dropped quickly to the creek and the open meadow of the valley bottom.

In this new world of Oklahoma the hills and slopes had been replaced with pancake flatness and dirt streets and little patches of concrete that had been, in the prouder days of this skidding trailer park, someone's patio. The trees of the Black Hills had been replaced with thirsty and mostly dead grass. The other Forest Service homes of my father's co-workers had been replaced with aging pickups, hastily hooked up travel trailers, and hammered motorcycles.

The arrival of harvest crews from various states had caused this little park to swell in human population and almost choke in battered metal mobile homes. Trailers were parked at odd angles wherever they could be jammed. Extension cords ran across dirt to the closest outlet. Sewer pipes had been taped together in makeshift fashion in order to get by for the eight to eleven days that a crew would be in town. Pickups and service trucks were double and triple parked. The park looked like a storm drain after a bad flood that had filled up with bikes, broken barbeques, wagons and real estate signs.

Parks like this would be my home for the summer. In each new wheat town our crew, and many others, would blow in with our rolling aluminum homes, jam them in any tolerable space, chock the wheels, cut our wheat, and quickly burn out to the next wheat town. In leaving we left behind the flotsam and jetsam of our trade: beer cans, broken lawn chairs, cigarette butts, worn out gloves, bags of trash, and watermelon rinds.

When it was time to move, the service truck was hooked to the trailer, the sewer pipe and hoses were thrown into the box of the truck, and the trailer was jerked out of its cockeyed slot. As you jerked the trailer out of its temporary place, a glance in the side view mirror revealed a combination of dump, lost and found, and compost pile.

It was almost 8:00 AM, and I could see no one stirring in the trailer court. At home I had to be up at 6:00 AM and on the road to school no later than 6:45 AM to make the twenty-eight mile drive into Rapid City in time for school.

The daily schedule of the wheaties was far different. Since wheat could not be cut and taken to the elevator until the moisture content dropped below about ten percent, wheaties slept in until eight or nine or sometimes even ten—all depending on the humidity of that day. Then we ate, gathered the crew, went to the field, serviced the combines and sometime after eleven, we began to cut. If the wheat stayed dry enough

37

we could cut until midnight or 2:00 AM. In fact, we cut all night on a couple of occasions when the humidity was real low and the boss was real anxious to finish up in a particular town and move on. I did not yet know this schedule and did not yet know to sleep until Don leaned in the trailer door and shouted at us for breakfast.

I had only walked a few steps away from the crew trailer, going nowhere really, when Don leaned out of his trailer and yelled, "Dave, come in for breakfast."

I turned and walked to the Dexter's trailer. The door through which Don had spoken was open except for the screen door. I pulled it open and stepped up into the trailer. The living room had been converted into a large dining room where all of us, the crew and the family of five, could all eat at once. Once, twice, or sometimes three times each day, the crew would traipse up the sagging metal stairs and invade this dining room for a meal. Don's wife had come to see these meals as a regularly scheduled invasion of smelly ruffians and clearly resented the intrusions. How she felt about preparing food for that many was also clear.

I was surprised to see that Dan was already up and sitting at the breakfast table. He too did not know the routine. He was eating pancakes and had a cup of coffee cooling in front of him.

"This is my wife Marie," Don said to me.

Marie came across from the stove and shook my hand. She was a pretty woman, about thirty-five years old, with brown hair down to her shoulders and, when she would allow it, a kind face. She seemed pleasant enough now. She may have been putting on her best mood for the new kids. Her outstanding feature was that she was taller than Don by an inch or more. She was also thinner than him by a foot or more.

Marie, whom the crew behind her back called "Helga," was the cook. Only Mark knew where the name "Helga" came from in the history of summers past. He would not say because it was one more piece of power over us to know the origin of something we did not. Marie was a nice enough woman, a decent cook and much too pretty to be married to a slouch like Don.

It soon became abundantly clear that Marie was also permanently unhappy at being a cook for a traveling harvest crew. Marie had not planned when she married a relatively prosperous wheat farmer in Oklahoma to be a cook for a traveling wheat harvest crew. She was not the first, nor the last, spouse to get into something that he or she had not planned on—and certainly would have avoided if the future had been known. The meals showed up on time and they tasted good enough. But they also showed up with the coldness of a woman who was not happy and was going to spread that unhappiness to anyone within striking distance. Don and all of us would pay all summer long.

As Marie and I processed our first impressions of each other, neither of us knew that this was my last year on the harvest crew and her last year on the earth.

"Nice to meet you," I said.

"Good to meet you, Dave," she replied. I was surprised that both Don and she already had my name down. "So, you are from Rapid City too?" she wondered.

"Yes ma'am. I go to the same school as Dan, but we didn't know each other until we both answered your ad," I offered.

"Well sit down and have some pancakes before the rest of the crew gets here," she instructed.

I sat down next to Dan who was already eating. The chairs had a flower pattern in faded orange or faded yellow or green. They were the cheap, padded, tired kind you get at a garage sale or cannot sell at a garage sale. The padding of the chair was starting to compress from what must have been hundreds of meals under the weight of various wheaties.

Marie brought me a plate of pancakes and sausages. They looked and smelled great. I was too timid to say, "This is too much." In my usual compliant way I began to eat and eat, tackling the meal like an obsessive compulsive with a new to-do list.

"Do you want some coffee?" she asked.

"No thank you," I said, "I don't like it."

Marie and Dan looked at me for the briefest moment and seemed like they were both going to smile but did not. It must have seemed mildly funny to them that I felt I needed to explain not liking coffee rather than just decline the offer of a cup. Don Dexter missed the entire interchange of whatever had just happened between the three of us. Don was at this moment gearing up for what he wanted to say to us.

"Listen," said Don, "Since you are both here already let me explain a couple a things about the work."

"First of all, I pay $1.50 an hour when we are cutting and 75¢ an hour when we are moving machinery. You can keep track of your own hours if you want, but I will be keeping track every day and you don't have to worry about it if you trust me to keep good numbers."

"There are lots of ways to get hurt in this work but the three biggest things to watch are fires, truck wrecks, and augers. You probably don't know this, but when you are driving trucks and pickups in the cut stubble, the straw tends to pick up on the mufflers and it can start on fire. You must check your mufflers all the time. Don't assume it's OK because it usually is not. Every time you have been driving in stubble for even thirty minutes, you just get out and pull the straw off the muffler. If you start a fire in a field and it gets into the standing grain, it will cost me a lot of money and it will cost you your job."

Don went on, "The other thing that you have got to be careful with is the augers. Never, never reach into those bastards. If they get plugged up just shut the machine down and then reach in there and pull out the stick or the rock or whatever is clogging it up. If you leave a machine on and reach into one of those augers, we will be sending you back to your mamma with one arm. And that same thing goes for belts. The belts on those combines will chew you up too. Keep away from them when they are running. They are flying so fast and you can't even hardly see them so just stay away from them. I had a little cocky kid one year who screwed around and tore up his hand real bad in a belt. It left a tendon hanging out and blood and screaming and a long drive to the hospital. They patched him up and sent him home to a hand doctor. And I had told the little punk too."

Dan was done eating, and I paused for a minute.

"Never drive crazy in my rigs or I'll fire ya," he said. "Simple as that."

"I'm gonna teach you how to unload the combines on the go so that we can save time, but I will have to show you that once we get out to the field," he concluded. "Oh," he added, "By the way, I don't know yet if I am going to put you two on trucks or combines or what just yet. I like to wait a little till I get to know a kid. Whatever I put you on you'll be on all summer. I don't like switching people off and on to different equipment. I get enough stuff tore up without guys changing around all the time on what they're driving."

By this time I was feeling very full and had eaten my sausage and most of my cakes. Dan was leaning back in his chair and nursing his coffee.

As Don spoke the door pulled open periodically and bleary eyed men and boys began to troop into the door at odd intervals. We were introduced to each one as they entered—first names only as that is all Don knew. The introductions were informal, and the responses to us were mostly indifferent but not curt. This was a wheat crew, and it was a morning after some had cut wheat late and drunk even later. The social atmosphere of our crew was one hundred eighty degrees out from a finishing school or a country club.

Don finished with his orientation, so I excused myself to get my duffel opened and find some clean clothes before we went to the field. I had barely changed and stuffed my dirty things into the duffel when it was time to load. I locked my duffel quickly and stowed it between a bunk and the shower wall. It was the last day that I worried about locking it.

We all piled into three rigs—Don's pickup with the open box, three guys in the Camaro, and the service truck with the metal cabinets—and headed to the field.

The Oklahoma landscape was new to me. Most of my life had been spent knocking around the Rocky Mountain West and I had seen very little of the flatness that allowed you to see all the way to a hazy horizon. I had spent some summer days at my uncle's farm in South Dakota, but the rolling hills of the short-grass prairie was pregnant with relief in comparison to this.

With each new turn and each swale and each mile I lost hope that I could find my way back to town with a load of wheat. Watching the route backwards as the wind blew across my burr cut hair, I was unable to keep track of all the turns. This fear of not being able to learn the way to and from dozens of back-road fields was one of the reasons that I was quietly hoping for a combine driving assignment. This circuitous route was the first of dozens and dozens that I would memorize and not think about over the next three months. The twisting path that had seemed so hard getting to that first field would become an easily remembered way. As we moved from field to field over the course of three months, the routes, while always new, became easy.

We left Lawton, drove on pavement for several miles, left the pavement and some miles later made a left into a half-cut field of ripe, blond wheat. The service truck and Don's pickup stopped in the stubble next to the combines. I climbed out with the rest of the crew.

Parked there in the field were four combines in a neatly staggered row right where they had been shut down in the great sweep of harvesting wheat. The first two were red diesel Massey-Fergusons with enclosed cabs. The last two were silverish gray metal Gleaners with open cabs. Off to the side, but in a jagged row, were four Ford trucks. They were all two-ton monsters with worn metal side panels to hold in the wheat and rolled-up tarps at the front that could be pulled over the load in case of rain or long trips to the elevator in town. Three of the trucks looked to be only a couple of years old, and the fourth was maybe ten years old. They all had the square-nosed look of a Ford, red paint, dirty wheels and huge side mirrors.

The other crew members went dutifully, though slowly, to their various tasks of checking belts, greasing zerks, checking oil, tying down tarps, checking tires, warming motors, and sloshing the worst of the dust off of windshields.

Dan and I did not know what to do, so we stood around awkwardly. I had no idea about this machinery or this work or what I should do. One of the interesting realities of ragged crews like ours is that you learn in a hurry simply by being shown and expected to do it from there on. I learned in a hurry, despite the fact that my "formal wheatie" education for the entire summer, accomplished over pancakes and sausage, was over.

When Don saw us, he called to us and said, "You two just wait a minute and I'll get you started." This would be our last morning for almost ninety days with nothing to do and we both sensed that. "I am hoping for a combine," Dan said and that surprised me. Dan did not strike me as a boy with the ability to spend hundreds of hours by himself on a combine in the dust and the sun and the boredom, with no audience, no variety, and no new scenery. After some delay I said, "Me too."

After Don finished with a stubborn, slow-starting combine he walked back to us and said, "Dan, I'm going to put you on a combine, and Dave, I am going to give you a try on a truck." Dan was glad and I was deflated, but we both knew better than to reveal it. Don probably assigned me to a truck because he correctly read me as a compliant kid, and he figured that I would come straight back to the field without a stop at the bar for a beer or at the Dairy Queen for a half-hour milkshake. He may have already read Dan and decided to keep him in eyeshot by keeping him in the field all day.

Whatever Don's reasoning for those assignments, they fit both of us. As the weeks wore on, I would be elated with my assignment; if Dan had any regrets about his, he never showed it. It became clear that I did far better with the variety of leaving the various fields and driving to the various towns and meeting the various drivers in waiting lines and the various clerks at the elevators. I thrived on the variety of a moving truck while Dan settled into the monotony of combine operation with an ease that surprised me. With a skill that I did not know he possessed, Dan climbed up every day onto his open cab Gleaner, started it and cut a straight swath right behind the Massey in front of him and right in front of the Gleaner behind him.

Adjust the header, set the speed, check the swath, check the level of the header, watch the gauges, keep up with the pace, put out your auger when you need to be unloaded, unload while going straight, turn right, go straight, turn right, go straight, turn right, unload while going straight, turn right, go straight, turn right, and go straight for an ever and ever shorter period of time and turn right sooner and sooner and then we are done with that one. One field done and who knows how many to go.

Dan was on his mindless combine acting in one famous play after another while I was in my truck making up plays as I drove along. In his mind Dan must have acted a lifetime of leading roles as he eased through the mindless days of "go straight, unload, and turn right." Most of my plays involved pretty cheerleaders and touchdown catches as time expired and me pulling various helpless people from burning cars and shooting Boone and *Crockett* Record Book Black Hills whitetails and saying clever lines I had thought up on the spur of the moment and delivered with a grin to a crowd of listening friends at the lunchroom table. Dan was playing the lead in Our Town and I was playing the lead in My Town and ten other guys, also mindlessly occupied, were playing the lead in Some Town, and in our fantasies we were winning at life. In your mind, alone in a dust blown and chaff-filled field, you can win every time.

This, my very first field as a wheatie, was big enough that Don turned all four machines loose to mow it down. Four combines staggered behind each other—each taking the next swath behind and beside the machine ahead of it. The four machines were capable of fourteen foot-wide swaths, and one pass down a field cut a combined swath more than fifty feet wide. When they were in sync and in stride, they were beautiful: four chewing headers, four clouds of dust and chaff, four whining engines, four sets of slowly rolling wheels staggered behind each other in lumbering alignment and powerful ease. I never tired of watching them.

Wheat harvesting was once a community affair where adjoining farmers worked together to harvest each other's grain. Each year everyone came together to help everyone—it had an Amish barn-raising feel and function. This was especially true in the days when harvesting required the intense labor of hand cutting, shocking and feeding wheat into threshing machines and shoveling cleaned grain. The "thrashing crews" were legendary for their long, hard labor and their ability to eat.

Gradually harvesting became less of a community event as machinery got more sophisticated and labor got less intense. There were many grandfathers who watched us roll into their fields who could remember the days of intense, prolonged physical labor to bring in wheat. Now our four machines harvested more wheat in a day than their community could do in a month.

Since their invention in the 1830's, the construction of combines has grown progressively more complex and sophisticated. They require, in every era of their evolution, adjustment and attention by someone like Don Dexter who knew how they worked and knew it well. There was plenty that could go wrong with a combine as it had "too many moving parts" to be sure. However, when a combine was working, it was a magical machine that took standing wheat and turned it into bushels of beautiful grain in a flash. In comparison to the ancient methods of hand thrashing and in comparison to the early methods of mechanical thrashing, the combine was a miracle machine.

The header of the combines had a fan which looked like a wide and squat paddlewheel off of a river boat and that bent the wheat into the cutter bar. The cutter bar was essentially a giant version of hair clippers that cut the wheat off. The motion of the combine moving forward and the motion of the fan pushing the wheat backwards laid the wheat on a chain driven elevator—a conveyor belt of sorts—that fed the wheat up into the machine and across a drum and bar set up which is called the thrashing cylinder. This mechanism beat the wheat out of the head. Then the kernel of wheat, being heavier than the straw and the chaff, dropped down through a grate and was augured up into the storage hopper. The straw and chaff were blown out the back end and spread by a fan called a chopper that looked like a huge ceiling fan.

In addition to improved machinery, individual farmers gained so much acreage that they bought their own combines and harvested their own wheat. With the expense of machinery and the even greater growth of some farms came the advent of the custom harvest crews. Many custom harvesters had wheat of their own in one state or another along their route. They cut from south to north, maximizing the investment in their expensive equipment and minimizing the expense of cutting their own wheat. For the many wheat farmers the expense of a combine could not be justified for cutting only your own wheat.

Community harvesting still happened here and there. Much more happened by individual farmers with their own machines or by wheaties like us, who rolled in with multiple machines, staggered them in a field and mowed it down.

Before my first chance to load a truck, an idler pulley broke on one of the Gleaners, and Don sent me across the field to the service truck for a wrench and a part. It was already hot, and the truck was half a mile away. It seemed to me that we should be in a hurry to get this work done, so I jogged in my new high top boots through the stubble to the truck and extracted the wrench and found the little plastic baggie with the part and jogged back with it. By the time I got back, the salty sweat was stinging my eyes and my shirt showed a path of sweat down the front and down the back. Don was clearly pleased and totally unaccustomed to having any wheatie exert himself beyond the bare minimum of effort. He thanked me and commented about my extra effort. As the sweat dripped down my face and ran down the middle of my back I felt good about Don already. The feeling would not last.

After the repair Don sent the driver back to cutting and said to me, "Let's teach you how to unload. I'm putting you in the old beast there."

"Fine with me," I said. We walked across to the oldest truck.

I would grow to love that oldest two-ton with her smooth-worn gear shifter and broken down seat and the familiar armrest and slick, skinny steering wheel and the split axle transmission that at first seemed like an unlearnable curse and later became an easy joy.

Old Red, when loaded, was a lumbering beast. The weight of the wheat made her feel worse than my dad's Ford Station wagon loaded with the whole family and our camping gear. My dad, frugal man that he was, always bought Fords with a straight six engine and a manual transmission. "Three on the tree," he would say, "is good enough for me." They were all reliable machines but could not outrun even a motivated calf. This truck was in the same class.

The inside of the old red beast would be my summer home. The face of the dash was a square, faded red. The top of the dash was brittle red vinyl that had cracked in multiple spider web patterns from countless hours in the merciless harvest field's sun. The radio was covered with dust but apparently worked. The cigarette lighter was gone. The seat was broken down. The windshield was cracked across the passenger side. The odometer was broken at 135,000 and change. I liked the rig immediately and was glad to have drawn an old, reliable steed. Old reliable things had begun to resonate with me.

I got in the passenger side and Don in the driver's seat. One of the Masseys had his auger out which meant that he was nearly full and needed to unload. Don started the truck and lumbered through the prickly stubble until he was driving the same speed as the combine and only a few feet off the left side of the whirling header.

"Now listen," he barked over the noise of the machine, "just ease up to the side of the machine like I did and keep a little distance away from the header. Then, when you are about this close, open your door and keep your right foot on the gas pedal and stand on the running board with your left foot. Keep both hands on the top of the wheel and look backwards over the cab so you can see right where the end of the auger is. Then start easing up to the side of the combine until the auger is right over the middle of your bed. You've got to keep pace with him and keep the same distance from him. Don't get into that header or I will be changing pulleys till Christmas. When you have the pace and the right distance, give the driver a nod and he will start the auger and empty his hopper. Best thing to do is just watch me."

With that Don threw open his door, stood up with his foot still on the gas and his hands still on the wheel and angled toward the lumbering combine. I could not see his shoulders and his head, but he was twisted back to watch the wheat unload into the bed. It looked pretty easy, and I was anxious to try. Don had probably done this a couple thousand times. A thing can be pretty easy for someone who has done it that much.

In reality unloading on the go, which most of the wheat crews did not do, may have saved a few hours over the course of a summer but cost much more in dollars and repair time. Rookies and veterans, who were screwing around, tore up plenty of machinery in the process and the net financial result was probably a wash. However, unloading on the go gave a sense of urgency to the work, and it was great fun for a kid who had never even driven a truck this big.

Don finished the task, pulled away from the combine, and sat down inside the cab again. "I'll let you try the next one," he said, "and I'll ride with you just in case."

That never happened. Don got busy on something, another auger came out, he motioned me to get it, and I started the motor. I tried to imitate what he had done. When I stood up to move in closer, I found that at six-foot and three-inches I could very easily stand in the position he had shown me, I could easily reach the gas pedal and the steering wheel, and I could easily see back to watch the auger. However, I had stood up about thirty feet away from the side of the combine. So, still standing, I began easing in toward the noise and the dust and the incessant vibration of the combine and the waiting auger. It took a long time but I finally got close enough and, palms sweating from anxiety, I nodded at the driver. He engaged the auger.

I looked back from my nod and watched the beautiful golden stream of wheat kernels flowing out of the auger, through the super-heated Oklahoma air, and into a growing, fluid pile of gold in the bottom of the truck bed. It was beautiful. I can still see that first stream falling safely into the bed. All summer long I relished the sight of the round flow of water-like wheat as it escaped the auger and piled in a spilling mound in the truck box. When the stream stopped I eased away, and the auger pulled back into the side of the machine. One down.

I peeled away from the line of combines and sat back down. Grabbing a higher gear I cut a wide arc around and back to my starting point for the next load. When I got back to my starting position, I shut off the truck. Another truck was turning into the field and coming to line up behind me. I felt a terrific satisfaction. I felt like a veteran. I felt like a team member who belonged and who could carry his own weight. The sum total of my contribution to the harvesting effort for that summer had been a one mile jog across a field and unloading one hopper. But I had done that much and I was ready to do more.

Off to my right the four methodical monsters were, in turn, turning right and moving off to the far side of the field. Atop each machine was a wheatie, silent in the kidney-jarring motion and the ear-splitting sound of the metal apparatus. Each man was making his header adjustments, checking his hopper level and his gauges, watching his speed and keeping his swath right and listening for the sound of the machine.

The sound of the machine was critical. Often, before a belt or pulley broke, a veteran could hear the machine make a complaining sound and shut down before the breaking. The veterans were doing this on autopilot, zoned into some other place and life. The rookies were still concentrating and fighting to remember everything and to turn right when they should and occasionally pushing a lever the wrong direction for the adjustment they needed.

I sat in my truck watching the progress. Another truck pulled into the field and the four harvesting hulks came back to my side of the field and two augers went out. I started my old red beast and drove off to take the lead load. Behind me another truck bounced along in my huge side mirror, angling his way to the second auger. It felt like I knew what I was doing. This time I got a little closer before I stood up. My palms sweated again. Two down. Grab a higher gear. Circle around. Shut her down. Wait.

Don hesitated next to me in his pickup and said, "I'm heading into Lawton for some parts. When lunch gets here, you can drive for one of the guys so he can eat. After you eat, you can take your load into that first elevator on the left as you come to town. Don't forget to weigh out and put the scale slip in the glove box." "Okay," I said as he drove off in a hurry. All the machines were running, and I was not sure what parts he needed. I didn't ask and later learned not to ask.

The set of instructions he gave to me were "first day instructions." I had always had a keen sense for what I needed to do next in order to move a project forward. From that day on I spent the summer working ahead of Don's instructions and anticipating the bottlenecks in our work progress. Don had never seen a wheatie like me in this regard.

I sat in the heat of the truck cab, then leaned against the box on the shady side, then walked around in the stubble with no pattern and no destination. In the dark corner of my mind was the lurking fear that I was getting out of shape and football season was already stalking me.

The machines lumbered past, no augers out, and the smell of diesel hit me again. That distinctive smell had already invaded my olfactory memory and was permanently embedded there. For the rest of my life, I would smell the diesel of a truck or a pickup or a motor home and would be transported back to these super-heated wheat fields of my sixteenth summer, when the whole world was shimmering in the mirage of the rising heat as I sat on the running board on the shady side of Old Red.

Before my next chance to unload, Marie arrived in the field with our lunch in the back of her massive Chevy Station wagon. The car was a dark green land yacht a little longer than Rhode Island. It was in desperate need of new shocks and moved like a heavy sled. She backed up next to the service truck and climbed out to open the tailgate. Her three kids got out and wandered around looking for something interesting. They were supremely bored and the summer was not even a third over for them.

Marie asked Mark where Don had gone. Mark lied to her and said that he had seen Don leave a little while ago but did not know where he was headed. Marie's stiff anger rose another notch, and she went about setting out the lunch in an angry hurry. I had been reading people's moods since I was 18 months old and I was already good at it. I could see the tension in her face and the speed in her walk and the exaggerated slamming of plates. Mark and I each drifted off to relieve a combine driver. Exactly the nature of the tension between Don and Marie was not clear to me, but it was clear that the tension was substantial and that Don had become a professional at not being where his wife was.

I climbed up the gray, hot metal ladder of a massive, idling Gleaner and sat in the hot seat. Even at idle the noise was deafening. Dan showed me the foot pedals and the levers and the gauges and said, "The header is at a good height. Just leave it alone. It's yours, weenie. Don't wreck my rig." It was the shortest and most inadequate orientation to a piece of machinery that anyone had ever received. A high school boy who had been driving a combine for three hours had oriented another high school boy on the operation of a $25,000 machine in about 155 seconds.

Dan jumped off the platform and fell in the dry stubble beside the machine. When he had picked himself up, he grinned at me in embarrassment and backed away. I was too anxious about my new assignment to even grin back. But I did think to myself, "Who's the weenie now, farm boy?" I was in the lead combine and clearly needed to get moving before the lunchtime replacement drivers behind me could get moving.

I mashed the clutch to the metal and moved the shifter into second gear. I looked behind me to see an impatient truck driver. I looked forward, engaged the header and watched the wide blades begin to rotate as the cutter head started clattering back and forth just three or four inches above the dirt. I eased up on the throttle and eased out on the clutch. Like most machines you must have a feel for the machine to make a smooth start. No two clutches are just the same. This clutch was not at all like Dad's Bronco.

The machine jumped forward like I had popped the clutch. Maybe I had. To my great joy it did not die and I was cruising down the field. I looked down to check my gauges and to adjust my speed a little slower. When I looked up, I had already veered into the wheat too far and was leaving a narrow, one-foot swath of uncut wheat out to the left of my header. I corrected the machine so quickly that I dipped the right corner of the header momentarily into the dirt. The cutter bar took a little divot of dirt and ground it up with a miserable clatter. The grinding sound didn't last long, and I kept on.

I had been in control of the behemoth for less than thirty seconds and had already popped the clutch, left some uncut wheat, and dipped the cutter bar into the dirt. It could be a long lunch hour.

For the rest of that hour I kept the machine moving in the clockwise direction, turning right at approximately the right times, and only dipping the header in the dirt once more. Some of my turns were too wide, leaving a crooked turn for the rest of the drivers, and some of my turns were too sharp, leaving too big of a triangle of uncut wheat at the corner. It would only be days until I would get the hang of it and run the machine almost mindlessly for my one hour lunch relief shift and one hour supper relief shift each day.

On lunch breaks, when I drove so one of the men could eat in the shade, I felt a part of a skillful team as we followed each other around and around. We were an amazingly efficient crew at cutting wheat given our raggedness when not cutting wheat.

When Dan came back to the machine, I left it idling for him, climbed down the ladder and said, "Your hopper is almost full but I didn't know how to put the auger out." "I'll get it," he shouted and climbed back up.

As Dan and his gray metal mount lumbered off, I walked across the growing stubble sea up to the back of Marie's metallic chuck wagon. On the fold-down tailgate she had ham sandwiches, potato salad and watermelon. There was a five gallon cooler of lemonade and a few remaining store-bought vanilla sandwich cookies. I took two sandwiches, a massive pile of potato salad, some cookies, and a glass of lemonade.

I was a naturally gregarious kid in most settings, but today it felt better to ease away from the rest of the crew and from the stewing Marie and her bored children. The addition of Dan and me to the crew, along with another couple of college kids just two days earlier, had freshly stirred the social edginess of the older guys. Men were dancing around each other and sizing each other up like new drifters in a bar. The Three Musketeers, who were the oldest and had been on the crew the longest, were making it clear that they had seniority when it came to lunch times and getting the good seats in the shade. I was too compliant, too much of an actor, and too little my true self to immerse myself in the dance.

I retreated to the shady side of Old Red. As soon as I got there, a little shot of adrenaline ran through me. I had already forgotten one of the two warnings from breakfast. After setting the plate and glass on the running board, I lay on my belly and looked under to check the muffler for straw. To my relief there was nothing on it. I had forgotten all morning to look even once. I turned back and sat on the ground against the massive rear outside dual and started on my lunch. I was much hungrier than I thought.

All the combines were across the ocean of standing wheat from me. It was as quiet as it could be with them anywhere in the field. I sat in the loneliness of my little piece of portable shade and thought about the day. I had slept in a borrowed bed, gotten my instructions for an entire summer's worth of work in less than five minutes, impressed the boss, witnessed the substantial tension between the boss and his wife, missed a swath of wheat, "oiled" the cutting bar of Dan's Gleaner with dirt and pebbles, and incorrectly shown myself to be a loner. It was only 1:00 PM and I hadn't even hauled my first load of wheat out of the field.

I finished my plate and returned the trash to Marie. She was gathering up the aftermath of lunch and anxious to leave. I began to feel sorry for the woman. Her misdirected anger had felt terrible, and normally I would begin to hate her. But, for reasons I did not understand, I felt bad for her. I could see some of the sadness of her circumstances, and I could see some of the suspicion in her eyes. At the same time I could also see how her own angry responses, gunned at anyone within range, complicated her life.

I returned to my truck and responded to the next signaling auger. When the river of wheat closed off, I eased away and looked at my load. It was maybe a little lower than Don had told me to fill the bed, but I was not going to risk a spill by unloading another full hopper. The drive to town was not too long and there was no rain in a nine state area, so I didn't need to tarp the load. I carved a wide turn back to the left and toward the gate.

When I left the field I tried to change the rear axle to high range instead of jumping up to the next gear. I had the engine at too high an RPM and the rear gear box ground bitterly. I slowed the truck and settled for the gear I had. It would take another week, and who knows how much metal shaving in the bottom of that gear box, before I got the hang of the split axle shifting. I kept trying.

I turned toward town. The windows were down and the breeze was hot but felt good in comparison to no breeze in a baking cab. I messed with the old radio until I got a station and eased down the gravel road. Back home in Rapid City, South Dakota, when I drove the Bronco back and forth to school I was listening to "Time of the Season," "In the Year 2525," "Build Me Up Buttercup," and "Bad Moon Rising." What came out of the crackling speaker in the top of the dash of Old Red was not in the same musical species as The Zombies and Creedence Clearwater Revival. It was not even in the same musical family, but I listened.

Old Red took her time to get up to speed as I worked through the gears. The speedometer needle shook violently at any speed and was slowly creeping around the round dial on the dash. Just when I was getting some speed, I had to slow down for another turn. Once on the pavement I coaxed her up to fifty and let her run there. Folks passed me. The truck lumbered while the hot wind beat the side of my face, and the edge of Lawton sketched itself on the near horizon directly ahead of me.

I found the elevator without difficulty and pulled up behind the last truck in line. The line was short and moving, and I was soon parked on the scale to weigh before dumping. I had gone too far and hung the front tires off the scale. The elevator clerk had to come out of his glass-enclosed office and shout for me to back up. He was not happy at yet another sixteen-year-old, baby-faced kid who could not even park a truck on a massive scale. "I could park a train on that scale, punk!" he shot as he walked back to his office to record my weight. I sat and waited for him. The scale, like all of them in the summer days ahead, rocked gently under the weight and the braked motion of the truck as I waited for the signal to move on.

Elevators got their name because they "elevated" tons and tons of wheat for storage in very tall bins. All the towns in wheat country had them, and many were "co-op" elevators meaning that a farmer was part of the cooperative wheat growers' association and they together owned or leased an elevator. A farmer would put so many bushels in the cooperative elevator and get paid for the same number of bushels when the wheat was sold.

I was waved on and moved forty yards forward to again wait behind the new Chevy two-ton ahead of me. The guy got out of his cab to walk back and chat with me, but the line moved right away, and he went back to his truck and stayed there. Within a few minutes I was being waved into the elevator, which I did with great caution as my two wide mirrors had little room on either side of the door, and came to a stop where the elevator operator wanted me. I had not only been avoiding the sides of the doors with my mirrors but keeping the wheels on either side of a deep, open hole in the floor where the wheat would be dumped.

Behind me a man shouted, "Let her go!" over the noise of augers and fans and wind and truck engines. I put the truck into neutral, set the parking brake, revved the engine and reached to engage the dump bed. Fortunately, before I engaged the dump, I remembered that I had not opened the sliding tail gate in the back. I let the engine idle down and went back to correct my mistake. Back in the cab I repeated my process slowly and eased the dump bed into the air. I could not see it, but behind me Old Red was vomiting out a beautiful torrent of wheat. It took less than a minute or so for all of it to flow out. A kid working for the operator reached in the bed with a scraper and pulled the little wheat that was left out of each corner. When he was clear, the operator signaled for me to lower the bed and move on.

The bed on Old Red came down slowly, and I let her get all the way down before leaving. I circled around the building, cranking hard to the right on the skinny wheel and hanging to the ruts in the dirt that a billion other trucks had made, and drove back to the exit scale. The trucks ahead of me were long gone, and I went right up on the scale, hitting it this time and weighed out. When the weight was done, the clerk handed a scale ticket through the window to me. I carefully placed it in the envelope in the glove box before starting back for the field.

One trip down. It had not gone without a hitch, but the hitch was minor and I was relieved. I retraced my route and got back to the field at about 5:00 PM. The machines had finished the whole field, save for my little one foot swath which one of the drivers was going for now. We were moving up to Kansas tomorrow. The wheat that Don had contracted for the Lawton area was done and I had only been there for one day of it.

Don was working feverishly to get the sides off one of the trucks and motioned me to take mine off too. He planned to load the machines tonight before we went in for dinner. It would mean a late dinner, but Marie would not have to bring it out to the field.

I worked next to Don, doing to my truck what he was doing to his. With a crowbar and great effort I wrestled with the box panels until they were all off the truck and stacked in a pile in the stubble. The combine operators were removing their headers and chaining them to long skinny trailers that someone had pulled up from the ditch near the edge of the field. One by one the trucks were backed into the ditch and hard against a makeshift loading dock of dirt.

As each machine was stripped of its header, Don would ease the combine up onto the flatbed of the now "boxless" trucks. Each combine weighed more than four tons, and the tires of the combines were so wide that they partially hung off each edge of the bed. Every machine had to be centered just right, and only Don or Mark were allowed to drive them on the beds. The Three Musketeers scoffed at this rule, but it was a rule that stuck all summer and they eventually stopped asking to drive the beasts up. Once on the truck, the combines were tied down with massive chains and tensioners that had to be levered over with a cheater bar made of pipe. Then the truck was returned to the field to pick up the side panels, chain them under the combine, and hook up the trailer with the header for that combine.

When the whole operation was done, the four massive combines were piggyback on four flatbed trucks and the four headers were in tow behind. The connected length of one truck and trailer was over forty feet. A combine on a truck looked like a garage on a pickup. It looked top heavy, and, I was soon to discover, it drove top heavy. The gentlest turn coming out the field, as easy as I was going, felt like the entire rig was going over and I drove the loaded double behemoth with a caution that bordered on ridiculous. On that first drive with a combine aboard, my palms were as wet as when the jet first lifted off in Rapid City.

In the morning we would hook onto the two trailer houses and roll. The four combine-toting, trailer-dragging trucks in one line, combined with the two trailer houses behind pickups, and Marie's Rhode-Island-sized station wagon made a caravan that was almost impossible to pass. The combined fuel consumption was frightening. Our collective fleet rolling down the pavement in that formation was using a gallon of gas every mile. Hopefully, Don had the ability to not think about that.

We got back to the trailers at 8:00 PM and went in for supper. Marie was not in a good mood despite the fact that we were going to their home place in Alva, Oklahoma, tomorrow and she would be in her own home for a couple of weeks. The kids were happy to be going home. Don was happy to be loaded, but he was exhausted.

Supper was not quite ready and as we sat down—the whole crew together for the first time since Dan and I had been there—the whole situation felt very foreign to me. I had met all the crew members but at the moment could remember only half their names. I did not know their personalities, bents, likes, histories or relative levels of interpersonal safety. I always hated talking to people without remembering their names.

I knew that Don and Marie were not doing the best in their relationship; for some reason this bothered me. Perhaps the rockiness of their marriage hooked some insecurity in me. Whatever the reason, I was, as usual, carrying concern for things that I had neither caused nor could fix.

That very first night eating together I observed something between Don and Marie. Don took off his sweaty and dirty shirt with the faded "Don Dexter Custom Harvesting" embroidery and held it out to Marie while he was looking toward the crew talking to someone. He expected her to stop cooking, take the shirt, and put it in the laundry.

Marie, who had clearly seen the extended shirt, ignored the shirt and continued what she was doing. Don continued his conversation, shirt hanging on his finger and held out to the side of him at arm's length, waiting for Marie to take the shirt. His undershirt was also filthy with sweat and dirt. The hanging rim of his belly slopped out below his sweat soaked tee.

Marie's anger was growing, and she did not take the shirt. Eventually, Don got annoyed that she had not taken it and turned to see why. She grabbed the shirt from his hand and disappeared down the narrow hall of the trailer. Every crew member on my side of the table saw the exchange and everyone was processing it—me with anxiety and the others with amusement.

Don's gesture of holding out the shirt seemed quite condescending to Marie. It was clear that he expected her to take his shirt, deal with it, keep cooking and not be thanked or even looked at while she did this for him. Clearly, Marie felt the condescension of it.

We ate spaghetti with meat sauce, salad, and rolls. There were ice cream sandwiches for dessert. Half the guys ate in a hurry and asked Don for an advance. Cash was doled out. Numbers were recorded. Slips were signed. Showers were taken. The Three Musketeers were in the Camaro and gone. They were closely followed by three guys in the service truck. The rest of us ate more slowly and one by one drifted back across to the crew trailer.

I was the last one to shower that first night. I was filthy and decided on this first day to break my vow of not showering for the entire summer. After everyone else had showered, I found some stout Ajax cleanser under the sink and scrubbed the shower floor as best I could. We as a crew were responsible to clean the shower in our trailer, but to my knowledge I am the only one who ever did. I heard other guys in the shower spitting great hunks of snot out on the floor and shuddered. Even scrubbing the slimy floor made me queasy. I scrubbed until I was sick. Although the shower did not look much better, psychologically it felt a little better. I got some clean clothes, turned on a pathetic little stream of hot water, and stepped gingerly into the little tin cage. The metal enclosure was so small that my elbows hit the sides whenever I tried to move or wash. In my mind I defied the laws of physics all summer by never really letting my full weight rest on the bottom. I showered in a hurry and stepped out onto my dirty shirt. One shower down.

So as it was, every night I braved the tiny shower—where hundreds of crew member showers had been taken complete with spitting, filth, and hair—and every night I stood on that slimy floor and hurried through a shower that I desperately needed if I were going to sleep. And every night I jumped out to rescue my poor feet from the mess they had once again endured. My perspective on my clean home was substantially changed when I got home that fall. But I was getting by.

It felt like it was going to be a long summer for me. I was a boy who had been in my fair share of dirt clod fights, cleaned plenty of fish, played army in muddy trenches, waded through many stagnant pools, covered my hands and face with grease from extended bicycle repairs, and worn a football practice uniform until it would stand up by itself. But when it came to lying down at night, I found that I needed to be clean and to sleep on something that was both clean and smelling clean—or I could not sleep at all. That adjustment was in high gear.

This cleanliness fetish of mine was helped by the fact that the crew trailer was one bunk short of being able to accommodate our crew. I happily volunteered to sleep on the extra cot that had to be set up somewhere outside the trailer at every stop. I would set up my cot in the place that seemed the safest, quietest, darkest and most likely to stay dry. If it looked like rain, I would search for some sort of overhang under a roof or trailer awning or a shed. A time or two I went to bed in the open, and rain came in during the night to soak me and send me running for cover with my cot and soaked bedding.

I got my used Army cot and my duffle bag. I set up the cot in a dark place in the shadows at the end of the trailer where I figured no one would be walking. I stowed my duffle under the cot, arranged my sleeping bag and pillow, and climbed aboard the rickety sleeping rack. It was my place and it was clean and I had control over it. I could sleep here.

I lay on my back in the cot and studied the darkening sky and the sagging power lines angling across the opening between trailers and the corner of the crew trailer and the occasional moth that had circled too far from the street light and the branches of an aging tree.

I was fitting into a custom harvest crew. I had worked for one day. I was satisfied that this day had gone well enough and that with some practice and some luck, I could do this job. So far, so good.

I was thinking about how hard it would be to actually sleep on this cot. The next thing I knew it was morning and sun was shining on my face. Another night down. Another eighty plus nights to go.

I registered that something in my anxious heart had calmed down a half notch. I knew where and when to get breakfast, and I had already been "trained" for my job. I was learning some of the names. I could unload on the go. I could park a truck on a scale, and I could tighten a massive chain with a cheater bar. I was under no illusion that I had mastered the summer's challenges, but I had survived the first ones, and for me the first challenges of anything were always the worst.

4 ALVA, OKLAHOMA

Just when you get situated,
It's often time to move again.

Don hollered into the trailer early. I doubt if many guys stirred inside the aluminum box. It was 7:00 AM, and Don wanted us to eat and roll. His machines were loaded and lined up. His wheat at home was ripe. Cutting wheat for others was important because they paid him for the work, but cutting his own wheat was paramount because the money from that crop was all his. He had called his neighbor and learned that his wheat was ripe. Urgency rose in his heart like a piece of steak choking him. His urgency drove him to drive us.

It would prove to be a frustrating morning for Don because the crew, when it finally did move, moved very slowly. It would prove to be a frustrating morning for me because I hated to see people in authority frustrated by people under their authority—even when it wasn't me causing the frustration. In my compliance I would be ready early, and in my need for compliance I would be anxious out of my mind because of those who had no need for compliance.

Most of the crew had been bouncing from bar to bar to bowling alley in beautiful downtown Lawton until 3:00 AM and beyond. I had heard the service truck come home first that night but did not go to the trouble of checking my watch. I heard the Camaro much later or just dreamed that I heard it. Some of the crew had been in bed for less than three hours.

I swung my feet onto the thin carpet of dying grass next to my cot.

Sleeping out in the open and waking up beneath the distant ceiling of the sky felt strange. As a kid in Cody, Wyoming, I had slept under the stars many, many times. Most summer nights a neighborhood sleep-over would come together just before supper. Friends were called and parents were cajoled and plans were made. In one of our backyards six or eight of us boys would throw sleeping bags on the grass, tell stories until our parents were asleep, and then begin to prowl the neighborhood for hours. We were a late-night pack of junior high boys out to raid gardens or throw eggs at a coach's pickup or TP a girlfriend's house. The point was always the thrill of adrenaline mixed with fear as we scaled fences in the dark, ran from dogs, dodged cars, ran through backyards, stole carrots and hid in bushes. We often ate raw vegetables in an alley just to feel that there was some other point to taking someone's garden stuffs. Sometime around three or four in the morning we would arrive back in the designated sleep-over yard, having bounced from garden to house to alley to backyard, and crawl into our sleeping bags and sleep until the sun was too hot to sleep anymore.

Even with all that experience of sleeping outside, it still felt strange to wake up and get up outside. There was no sense of defining the space where I was living. There were no boundaries and definition of how far I could go and others could not go. Fearful as I felt being exposed out in the open with no boundaries and no locks it still felt better to sleep on my cot with clean bedding and a bedroom as big as the universe. My duffle was stowed under the green canvas ship on which I sailed through the night. Even if my sleeping place and space moved multiple times throughout the summer, I greatly preferred the clean and controllable outdoor space to the stuffy, hot, and odor-filled trailer.

I got up and snuck between the trailer and a tree to relieve myself. This summer, and every summer of my childhood, and several others as a firefighter for the National Park Service, were times for outdoor relieving. It is a skill to relieve yourself and not be seen. I became an expert. I quickly broke camp on my little private bivouac. No one was moving in the trailer, and I stowed my gear in the service truck and headed towards the Dexter's for breakfast.

On the way to the trailer that morning I was embroiled in a debate with myself: my frugal self fought fiercely with my happy-go-lucky self over the question of buying some cowboy boots. The purchase would require a draw of about forty dollars on my pay, but I hated to spend the money. In fact that would be most of the money I had earned so far, but for reasons I do not understand I really wanted a pair of cowboy boots. Maybe the boots would confirm that I was a real cowboy and was out on a real adventure and was really on my own and could ride a real horse (if I had one) and was truly launched into the real world of work and competition, as opposed to the sheltered world of school and sports and living with my parents.

By the time breakfast was over my frugal self had won and I asked Don for a twenty dollar draw.

"What do you want that for?" he wanted to know.

"Just for some snack money," I said, "I don't have any money left from my trip."

"I'll give it to you but I don't want you drawing out everything you make like most of these yahoos and going home with nothing to show for a whole summer of work," he said with firmness but also with general kindness.

"I don't want to do that either," I assured him. He gave me the twenty in a single bill and had me sign a little slip to verify that I had taken the draw.

I left the trailer wondering what had just happened. Don had clearly taken an interest in me and wanted something better for me than the majority of his crew were choosing for themselves. Most of them would get to the final day somewhere in Alberta and settle up with Don and not have enough gas money to get back to Kansas. In an aloof way it felt like he was looking out for me. It also felt like I was a kid thrown back in Cody who was being told that he could not spend his paper route money on a football.

I put the twenty in my wallet with my driver's license and my social security card. The wallet was very thin. It was one of the wonderful carefree kid's wallets unlike adult wallets that get fat with plastic cards holding numbers that some clerk or receptionist or teller perpetually wants to see. Life's cares grow in proportion to the girth of a man's wallet.

Don put me to work on the details of getting loaded. By 11:00 AM everyone was up and fed. The trailers were hooked up, the extension cords were thrown in the back doors, the sewer pipes were stashed in the pickup box, the chocks were pulled, the turn signals were checked and the Don Dexter Custom Harvest Crew and Makeshift Rolling Metal Parade was ready to roll out of Lawton. We had no parade permit. Our kind of parades were common enough and were only a mild nuisance until our parade caught up to and attempted to pass another custom harvester's parade. Any tourist in a station wagon had better find another road or face the daunting task of passing a thousand feet of lumbering metal elephants.

There was no straight shot from Lawton to Alva. Our parade snaked out of Lawton, attempting to stay together, and turned north. We began a long, meandering day, slowly but steadily closing on the Dexter farm outside of Alva, Oklahoma.

I was alone in the cab as other wheaties who were not driving had opted to ride with someone else. I was happy about that as I still was not good at shifting the split axle and preferred to be alone as I improved my driving skills and shaved additional gear metal off the already worn gears. The top-heavy old Ford was a chore to drive on these two-lane narrow blacktop roads.

The pavement was hot and soft. There was little shoulder and no room for error. It was the kind of driving that required constant concentration to watch the distance from the combine trailer ahead of you, watch the mirror for passing cars and for problems with the header trailer, and watch the gauges for signs of overheating or low oil pressure. Most nerve-grating of all was to watch your place in the lane so that you were not in danger of crossing the center line or dropping a wheel off the pavement and into the ditch. Every dip in the road and buck of the pavement sent the collected rig, truck, combine and header trailer swaying, bouncing, bucking and heaving in a top-heavy, lurching, shock-absorber-stretching wave. This was all compounded by worn shocks, worn steering mechanisms, and worn brakes. The driving was work and the work was nerve wracking.

We ate a late lunch at a café in some little farm town. Our crew overwhelmed the "not used to lots of folks at once" system, causing the meal to take a long time to arrive. Don had instructed us not to spend more than five dollars apiece and made it clear that anything over that amount was coming out of our pay. I got into a rut of eating cheeseburgers, fries, and a vanilla shake for almost every one of our very few restaurant meals. Meals that Marie had not prepared cut into the profit margins, and Don worked hard to see that they were few. Today he would have to feed us twice on the road.

When we climbed back into the trucks after lunch I had an added battle to the difficult war of safely piloting my metal behemoth. The cheeseburger hit the bottom of my stomach and it added to the hot wind blowing in on my face and the miles of identical fields and the fence rows piled together in a monotonous string. I got sleepy. My eyes began to droop, and occasionally my head nodded for a moment as I fought the terrible sleepiness and lost track of my mirror, my following distance, my gauges and my driving line in the soft black overheated north-bound lane. More than once I came to consciousness when my head bobbed down. Finally, after three or four of these episodes, I came awake with both right wheels off the blacktop and fully in the grass of the ditch.

My father had drilled into my head that I should never jerk the wheel to overcorrect. I remembered his drill. I gripped the wheel and fought to ease my leaning behemoth back onto the road bed. I let off the gas and eased on the brakes. The truck slapped down huge weeds with its front bumper and spat gravel in long, arching sprays out across the barrow pit. I was very awake now. I eased old red back on the road.

Passing any vehicle that was moving faster than a bicycle was out of the question in my aged and overloaded truck. Pressing the foot pedal to the floor only raised the whine from under the faded red hood as she fought to accelerate. It would have taken twenty miles to pass a vehicle, so I crept along in line and periodically got hung up behind an even slower rig than my own. In those cases, I just waited until he turned off or pulled off to let me pass.

The sun fell in its steady arc to our left and dusk fell in on us. I turned on my lights and watched as sets of lights began to come at me in a spasmodic stream. My bug-spattered windshield with the slanting rays of last light added up to terrible visibility. The dusk deepened and I came into the time of day that I most hated driving. It was too dark to see well and too light for the headlights to do much.

We eased along even slower in the menace of dusk and poor visibility as the headlights could not overcome the half-light. Night driving was not much better. As oncoming headlights hit the slanted and filthy windshield glass, the definition of where the road actually turned and where the obstacles lay became more and more uncertain. At one point a dog crossed behind the trailer in front of me and my front bumper. It shot through the narrow stream of dirty light in a flash and rocketed out into the darkness to my right. The net effect was like a baseball pitched in one cab window and sailing out the other without touching anything. No harm was done except for whatever harm results from a vicious spike of adrenaline and an instant rise in heart rate.

Sometime after eight in the evening we pulled into another greasy café where I had another cheeseburger, shake, and fries. Our crew was more subdued than usual as the tedious driving and the slow crawl had been wearing on everyone. Marie was sullen and her kids were whining. Don was quiet. Something had happened between the two of them for the fourth time in the young summer.

During dinner I kept my head down to read and reread the history of the little burg where we had landed as it was proudly printed on the placemat now stained with catsup. This was one more dying farm town that had seen prouder days many decades earlier and had, in the minds of some severely optimistic founders, been destined to be the next Denver.

With nearly fifteen people at our tables, two girls, both nice and in their teens, waited on us that night. One of them was very outgoing and flirty. The crew took to her of course. She was teasing and touching; who knows the motives that fueled the outgoing style? They may have been sexual, financial, theatrical, or all three.

The other girl was far quieter though not exactly shy. She was not pretty in the supermodel sense, but she was very attractive and probably more so because she seemed to me to be both confident and quietly humble. She had much more personal confidence and willingness to be who she was and not perform for others. She was also kind. I found myself looking at her almost continually. I had the curse of falling in love with girls in the space of 28 minutes, and I accomplished that with this girl—without ever speaking a word to her.

When both waitresses were gone from the table a spontaneous "vote" happened over which one was the more attractive girl. Only Marie and I voted for the quiet girl. Of course, I never saw her again.

We finished supper and scattered to our various trucks. It was only an hour to Don's place. Sometime after 10:00 PM our lumbering caravan snaked into the farm yard of the Dexter farm outside of Alva. It was dark. There was no way to see the lay of the land or to judge the prosperity of the Dexter place, and the yard light was insufficient to illumine the territory where we would circle the tin wagons. Marie and her kids disappeared into the dark farmhouse while Don jockeyed the trailers into a space between two sheds. Tired men bumped around in the dark, cussing as they stumbled over tree roots and rocks and hooked up the extension cords. Sewer pipes would wait until the morning. It was a makeshift hookup and no one cared. The crew was in no mood to head to town and was soon all filing into the trailer.

I pulled my cot and duffle from the back of the service truck and caught Don before he headed into the house.

"Where should I set up my cot?" I asked through the darkness.

"There's a big equipment shed right there," he pointed into the darkness, "and it's empty. Put your cot anywhere in there. The light switch is just inside the sliding door on the far side."

"Where's the door?" I asked in anxiety.

"Just around on the other side," he barked in tired frustration and disappeared into the dark.

Easing along slowly, I made my way to the huge metal shed and around the side into even greater darkness and felt along the wall until I found the sliding door. It was a massive and heavy door, and it took some trouble to coax it open. I reached inside to grope around for the switch which lit a single bare bulb hanging from the rafters in the middle of the shed. Her walls were tin and her rafters were cobweb-laced, dust-encrusted two-by-eights. Her floor was cracked concrete and in the middle, near the bare bulb, was a single center post, an aging eight-by-eight. She must have felt like she was holding up the whole world. Around the edges the shed harbored various storage shelves, hand tools, work benches, cobwebs and oil drums. She was empty of any machinery on this June night.

I carried my cot and duffle to the center post, set up the cot, spread out my sleeping bag, hung my clothes on odd nails in the center post, and walked back to the sliding door to douse the light. Once the sliding door was pulled shut, I cut the light and stood for a moment in the pitch dark. I was wearing only my underwear and standing on a cold concrete floor. I waited for my eyes to adjust to whatever light was going to be available through the two windows, but nothing much improved. After a long, or seemingly long, wait I headed across the concrete in the darkness in the general direction of my cot. I would have missed it if I hadn't kicked one of my boots as I was passing.

Once on the cot I waited longer in the darkness for my eyes to adjust. Slowly I could detect a small bit of light from one of the windows. I hated sleeping in pitch dark— I always wanted some sense of bearings, some way to know which way to the door, and some way to orient myself if I awoke in the middle of the night. Having tried to orient myself to the door and having tried to coax a little light to come in the window would be of no help in the near miss that was coming to me in just a few hours. Tonight, my first night in this cavernous machine shed turned bedroom, was to be my most frightening night of the summer.

I closed my eyes, listened, and thought for a long time about the new place and the summer so far and what sounds out there in the blackness might be unfriendly. I was anxious from the near miss of the ditch experience and almost surprised that we all made it across those ribboned miles of soft, hot asphalt. I was tired from fighting the loaded truck and weaving trailer. As the sounds became familiar, my anxiety subsided. I thought about the quiet girl and drifted off. The repetitive motions from the daytime driving followed me into the night and invaded my dreams and plagued me all night. It was not restful sleep. As if sleeping in a hot wind, I drove the top-heavy old Ford all night, weaving and lurching down curving miles of blacktop in a lumbering line of dreamed-up trucks, passing cars, darting dogs, vibrating mirrors, and heat mirages.

Sometime in the darkness of the middle of that night I woke up soaking wet. My sleeping bag was thoroughly soaked. I did not move as a depressed fear swept over me that I had, at the age of sixteen, for the first time in more than a decade, wet the bed. I was confused and sad and angry at the same time.

Worse yet, I was not happy about getting up in the pitch dark again and crossing the concrete to the wall and groping for the light switch, but I had no choice. I had to see what had happened and clean it up before my crew members got wind of anything. If I had really wet the bed and the word got out on the crew, I was in for a summer of misery and then Dan would spread the word back in Rapid City and I would be the target of ridicule forever. It would make the yearbook, and at the fiftieth reunion, which I would not attend for certainty of being ridiculed, they would still be talking about "that kid who wet the bed the summer of our junior year."

I crawled out of the soggy sleeping bag, put my feet on the cold floor, and began the dreaded trek across to the light switch. I had no idea of the time. It was still fully dark. I kept my hand in front of me, my feet getting colder and colder on the concrete. Finally, I hit the wall and groped along it to the switch and lighted the single dirty bulb above my bed.

I turned to make my way back and investigate my soggy problem, but froze in a heart-pounding terror. My heart went from a barely awake resting rate to the highest fight-or-flight rate in a second.

There between me and my cot, squarely on the very route that I had just traversed, was a rattle snake. It was big, vile, and ugly. Winding fast across my path, it slithered to my right and headed straight for the wall. A shudder of fear and hatred ran through me.

I have feared and hated snakes since I knew what they were. This terror and intense hatred was in total contrast to my brother who loved them and chased them and caught them and played with them and always wanted to keep them. Why would two brothers who came out of the same womb just twenty months apart take such a starkly different approach to snakes, and to eight dozen other things?

The snake had clearly not been there seconds earlier when I came across searching for the light, or I would have stepped on it. But it could not have been far from my path when I shuffled barefoot and bare legged across the concrete in the dark. Now it was right on my path.

I had no tool or weapon, and I was wet and scared and angry. There was nothing to do. I thanked God as I watched it go hissing all the way to the wall and out a hole under a workbench. Within minutes that hole was gone for good—as if there were not dozens of other holes remaining.

With my heart still pounding, I made my way back across the cold concrete, across the snake path, and back to my cot. The cot and bag were soaked beyond what a single bladder, especially a monumentally small bladder like mine, could have soaked it. I looked up to see a hole in the tin roof squarely above my cot. It had begun to rain in the night, it was still raining gently, and I had cleverly positioned my cot directly under the only leak in the entire shed. The rain had come in the hole, soaked my bedding and cot, and made a rug-sized puddle under my cot as it leaked through the saturated bedding and onto the floor. The rain had also driven the snake into the dry of the shed.

My spirits soared. I had not wet the bed. I had not been struck by a rattler in the dark. I knew where the leak was. Three great things in two short minutes! It was a great recovery from a miserable and frightening night.

I hung my soaked sleeping bag on a nail and moved the cot to the other side of the post. I got into some dry clothes and put a dusty rug on top of the cot. Thankfully my pillow was dry. With the light on and in my clothes, I lay down again and, in my exhaustion, went back to sleep—a sixteen-year-old on an adventure who had just averted not only terror but disaster and who was gently unconscious under the slight swaying of a dirty, 60-watt night light—driving a lumbering red truck through the night.

In the morning I turned my bag inside out and hung it up again. I made sure that the snake hole was well plugged with mechanic's rags.

The gentle rain continued. On the first day at Don's home place with wheat waiting, we were rained out.

I had breakfast by myself as Marie had set out cereal in their trailer and none of the other men were up. Easing back across the farm yard to my shed, I could see that the Dexter's place was older but both big and nice. The Dexters must have inherited a family farm because the place was not new, and Don, at only thirty-seven or thirty-eight years of age, could not have built the house. Still, the buildings and layout made it clear that this was a prosperous place.

Up at the farm house Don was frustrated because he could not cut. He told me that he was going to town for some errands and that we were not going to work that day. I could do whatever I wanted. Unfortunately, the options were limited since I had no car and walking around his farm in the rain was not appealing. Even less appealing was spending the day in the pickup with Don as he ran from Cenex to Ford Tractor to grocery story to drug store to tire store to grain elevator. I did have a book in my duffle bag, so I headed back to my shed to check on the drying of my bag and read my book.

I was not yet a reader due to very low personal patience and discipline and even lower reading speed. Reading for an hour was a major feat for me, and I had done that probably only five times in my life. I began to read, lost interest, made myself keep reading, got sleepy and put the book on the floor and slept in the middle of the morning.

Lunch was sandwich stuff set out in the trailer and a couple of crew members were eating when I got to the trailer. We talked a little, but they were nearly done eating. Some guys were not even up yet. I finished alone and wandered back to the shed.

As the sky was lighter now, I was afraid we might have to work after all, but the wheat was far too wet. I retreated to my cot. This time I only lasted a few minutes before I put the book down and began to tour the shed, moving around the entire outside wall, examining the contents. Boredom was driving me hard.

Outside the Camaro fired to life, and I surmised that the Three Musketeers were heading to Alva to get an early start on their drinking, fighting and skirt-chasing—if indeed Alva was big enough to support those activities. The three of them drove in the Camaro when we moved the machines any distance and they rode in the Camaro to town at night and they rode the Camaro whenever they could. Gary always drove. Kerry always rode shotgun. Tim always climbed into the tiny back seat.

Gary, Kerry and Tim had been best of friends since junior high in some little burg in Oklahoma. The snatches of information I gleaned from them so far made it clear that they were best of friends because they were partners in crime—some mischievous, some malicious, and some illegal. In their early teens they were attracted to each other as they kept meeting at the fire alarm to pull it or kept meeting in the principal's office because they had pulled it.

That early association became a legacy of trouble and fighting and drunkenness that by now had lasted more than two decades. In the course of those two decades, they had hung together, and they hung together tight. By the time they joined this combine crew they had collectively lost track of the number of times they had been fired, the number of cars they had wrecked, the number of kids they were not supporting, the number of fights they had been in and the number of debtors they had stiffed. In all that change, instability and self-destructive behavior, the one thing they had managed to not destroy was their friendship with each other—it was their one constant. They were still tight and viewed themselves as a modern day gang. Albeit, it was a gang without any notoriety, skill or real purpose other than having what they defined as a good time. They had one horse, a nice Chevy Camaro, a couple of guns, no money and no plans.

Gary was the least irresponsible of the three men which is certainly to "damn him with faint praise." He had applied himself to some job long enough to get a car and the other two had become his followers in some small way. He was generally likable when he wanted to be and treated me well enough. He struck me as a person who in his heart wanted a better life than his choices had afforded, but who had so little self-control that it never panned out. His main fault was a severe streak of deceptiveness that would rear its head periodically during the summer. If Gary could make his life better through some deception or another, he was more than willing to do that by lying or leaving out a detail or taking something. He was smart enough that most of his deceptions worked, but Don was also smart enough to know that things were happening. Either he did not have time to investigate Gary's crimes against his custom harvesting business, or he figured the losses were too small to worry about. Don needed combine drivers—even deceptive ones.

Kerry was Gary's "lieutenant" in this gang and was the most dangerous and malicious of the three. He was very thin with thin arms and various tattoos. His face was very gaunt and his hair thinning. He smoked continually and drank hard and chased women and fought often and had a generally mean exterior which fairly well matched his interior. Living hard had taken a big toll on Kerry—physically he looked horrible—yet there was a remarkable toughness in his body and inner determination. He did not acknowledge me when we passed in a field or in the trailer, and I stopped greeting him. He was the only crew member I felt the severe need to avoid.

The full-blown follower of the three was Tim. How he ended up with these two men is less clear. He was plenty irresponsible but certainly did not seem malicious to me. He had red hair, a rounded face and a pleasant manner. He didn't seem to fit with the other two, but had been with them for so long that he came harvesting with them and readily piled in the Camaro whenever they were going anywhere. For now they were gone to Alva or the nearest bar.

In my boredom I decided to investigate my shed-turned-cavernous-bedroom more closely. The walls of the shed were made of two-by sixes which were exposed on the inside and covered on the outside with corrugated tin. The exposed wood was tired, dirty, occasionally twisted and often cracked. Everything was covered with dust and most things were also wearing some amount of grease and cobwebs.

I toured the shed, slowly viewing every foot of every wall. The tour gave clear evidence that a very organized, diligent person had started well and was winning the fight with the ever-creeping chaos, then had become overwhelmed by work, urgencies and needs elsewhere and was for a fair stretch of time fighting to keep up and was now, at last, bitterly behind and fully resigned to the chaos. The evidence lined the walls of the shed like an over-stuffed museum. The museum contained literally hundreds of tools and parts and supplies—some broken and some new, some full and some empty, some serviceable and some ruined. It was a fascinating visit to what could have been the "Farm Shed Museum" for all of America. For nearly an hour I was a farm archeologist, lost in a major discovery.

This was my bedroom. I smiled at the thought of my mom saying, "David, clean your room!"

I finished my tour and went back to my cot to read.

Marie leaned in the shed and shouted for Don. When her eyes adjusted to the relative dark, she saw me and said with a scowl in her voice, "Have you seen my husband?"

"He left a couple of hours ago to get some parts," I said as mildly as possible so as not to further upset her.

It did not work. She snorted an angry, "Ya!" back at me and wheeled and left. I sat on my cot feeling guilty and wondering what I had done and why this woman was on such an incessant war path against her husband and against any other man within bitching distance.

The rain had stopped and the clouds were breaking. Don returned from town and I was thankfully not privy to the interaction with his wife when he returned.

In the morning the sky was clear and soon the farm was hot and steamy. Don watched the moisture content of his wheat religiously, and the moment it was dry enough we began cutting. Four combines eased around in ever decreasing rectangles until a given field was done and then moved immediately to the next field. Don had his own storage at the farm, so our truck runs were short and our wait in the field was longer.

Don seemed pleased with the yields, and we had it all cut in three days including breakdowns. With his wheat safely inside we began to move to other fields in the Alva area. As in most little towns everybody knew everybody. Don worked all his connections and got more acres here, naturally, than elsewhere—not because we were driving faster but because we had wheat lined up ahead of time. We stayed busy for the next two weeks—very busy.

From my few interactions in town, Alva seemed like a friendly place. It was a typical small town that had a weekly newspaper but did not need one. You could spill your coffee in the café and have the barber know about it before you got there for your haircut an hour later. It was also a place that seemed tired to me. I had no idea when it was founded or whether it was on the upswing or the downswing. It was probably on the "hold-your-own swing."

Many of the little towns where we landed on our wheat odyssey were on the downswing. As the mechanization got better, and the farms got consolidated, and the kids left for college in the city, the towns began to shrivel. It was a slow shrivel to be sure but over the years and the decades the accumulated effect was severe. Stores slowly went under and the buildings went for sale and finally just got boarded up. Farm implement dealers pulled out of the little dying towns. Newspapers closed. Schools got consolidated and kids got bussed long distances. A three-café-town became a one-café-town. Old-timers sat in the one remaining café every morning and drank coffee and ate cinnamon rolls and lamented the losses.

I was getting to know the crew better by now. My favorite wheatie on our crew was Cliff. He was another high school boy who lived near the Dexters and was traveling with Don's crew for the first time. Cliff was about six foot tall and very stout. He looked like he could have picked up a calf and carried it a hundred yards. His years of farm work and wrestling and football had molded him into a gentle giant of a kid. His face was angular but kind. His hair was thick and unruly though he did not care.

Don looked out after Cliff even more than he looked out for me since he knew the family and certainly did not want to face Cliff's mom and dad if Cliff got injured or landed in jail. While I liked Cliff, it was impossible to be his friend—I tried. Cliff was perhaps the most self-contained person I had ever met. He would speak to anyone who spoke to him, but he had no need to start a conversation with anyone. He rode his combine in silence and ate in silence if others would let him. He hung to himself. He just did not need anyone or was so afraid that he stayed away from everyone.

Dan remained friendly enough. We had flat nothing in common, but gave each other the thin moral support of having come from Rapid City together. He had no other real friends on the crew but everyone seemed to like him. In fact, except for the Three Musketeers there were no real friendships formed on the crew. Some guys were loners and some didn't think it worth the effort to become friends with guys they would never see after a few weeks from now.

The Three Musketeers viewed me as a "goodie-goodie" and told me so often enough when they derided me for not heading to town with the others. My inhibitions and fears prevented that trip, and I was happy enough in my condition. The ridicule got easier to take as the summer wore on.

I was seeing in myself a growing struggle between my inhibitions and my curiosity. A piece of me wondered what all went on between 10:00 PM when the Camaro left and 3:00 AM when the Camaro returned. I had an idea what went on, but certainly it was a vague idea—perhaps bearing little resemblance to the stark reality of those five hours. Sometimes, at the breakfast table Gary and Kerry would try to describe in detail what had gone on the night before—only to be stopped by Mark or Don. Mark hated their behavior, and Don hated for his kids to hear about their behavior.

The time in Alva went quickly—too quickly for me. I liked my tool shed bedroom and I liked the area and I liked not having Marie around as much as we so often made our own meals in their trailer while she and the kids were in the house or bouncing around town. It felt like I was off to a good start. The middle of the trip was going to be rougher than the beginning or the end.

I began to believe that I could do this, could survive this summer and maybe even enjoy parts of it. I had now survived two locations and moved well past the worst days of adjusting to harvesting, a new crew, a new living arrangement and being away from home.

5 DODGE CITY, KANSAS

Perseverance is not the answer to
everything in life,
but it is the answer to a lot.

In a past century Dodge City, Kansas, was famous for being a wild, violent and dangerous frontier town. The name conjures up pictures of desperados, gunfights, hangings, gangs, vigilante posses and wild saloon brawls. It was nicknamed "The Wicked Little City." It was the setting of the TV show *Gunsmoke* and the stomping grounds of Bat Masterson and Wyatt Earp. But in the summer of 1969, a wheatie sitting in the cab of an aging Ford and baking his brains out didn't see much of the violence and danger of the Wild West. I didn't see Bat or Wyatt or Matt Dillon, or any of the legendary wickedness. I imagine there remained plenty of wickedness of various descriptions to be found in Dodge City, but I mostly saw wheat, stubble, and the faded dashboard of a tired truck, and augers swinging out that said, "Get your butt and your truck over here."

Most of the stops on our five-state, fifteen-hundred-mile odyssey in that summer of 1969 were windy. The flat plains of these places that grew wheat and had suffered through the dust bowl have little to slow the wind. A quality tree belt does certainly help an individual farmstead, but no one can build a tree belt big enough to help a state.

Dodge City was no exception to the wind problem. I had lived in Cody, Wyoming, for four years before this summer and living in Cody had taught me to hate wind. My summer as a wheatie took that hatred to a new level. When the wheat was ready to cut the rain and humidity were usually down, often allowing a hot wind to blow across the region and be especially steady and hot in whatever field we were cutting.

The wind in Cody was relentless. It could be bitter cold or gusty or both. But it was never as hot as the wind of a Kansas-wheat-field kind of hot. Hot wind outside of Dodge City could turn an entire field into a dry sauna. The relentless blowing heat took moisture out of everything and the energy out of me. It was too hot to sit inside the truck with the windows up and with them down the cab became a mini wind tunnel. I spent many hours leaning against the rear duals in the shady side of Old Red—if I could see the combines from there.

A combine churning through standing wheat would stir dust which the wind was only too happy to drive into the eyes, ears, mouth and whatever other crack it could find in a wheatie. Even more miserable was the chaff and straw that was spit out the back of the combine. The chaff itched badly! I couldn't scratch it enough and I couldn't stop thinking about it.

As the thrashing process was completed inside the hot metal combine, the chaff and straw were spit out the tail end of the machine and hit a huge horizontal fan, called the chopper. The chopper scattered the tailings more or less evenly behind the machine. The hot wind eagerly picked up the stream and drove it everywhere.

By the end of a day, or well before, the mixture of straw, dust, and chaff was under all my clothes and inside the truck cab and down in my lace-up high-top hiking boots. My entire body would itch the way your neck itches when you have just had a haircut and little pieces of hair stick to you.

The heat and dryness of this wheat summer exacerbated another problem: my frequent nose bleeds. I had been susceptible to nose bleeds my entire life due to a bone spur in one nostril that had only a thin layer of skin stretched over it. I would just be sitting there and blood would start flowing out of my nose—it was on my shirt and pants before I could pinch my nose shut. Several times I would be driving up to unload a combine while standing on the running board, steering with one hand, and pinching my nose shut with my hankie with the other hand.

My problem with dirt and grime was compounded by the fact that for the first time in five years I had let my hair grow out. It got longer and longer and was so thick it was hard to wash, especially when I was trying to wash quickly while I levitated off the floor of the filthy shower.

I was a jock—not a talented jock or even a hard-working jock—but a jock nonetheless. Our coaches required burr haircuts for every athlete, for every sport. No exceptions and no discussion. The athletes in our school stood out like enlisted Marines at the movies.

I went out for every sport: football in the fall, basketball in the winter, track in the spring, baseball in the summer. So, for the past five years I had worn burr haircuts—which I hated. I determined that this summer, missing the baseball season, I would not get a haircut. Beyond that I decided not to wear a hat and simply let my hair bleach out as white as it would. By the time we hit the middle of Kansas, at the end of June, I was starting to make some progress on these simple goals. The respectable amount of hair I had grown in the past month had bleached from brown to beyond blond—almost pure white.

Sitting in the truck with my nose pinched closed with a blood-soaked hankie, hot wind blowing on me, chaff itching everywhere, my hair feeling greasy, trying to watch for extended augers, and a head aching from the sun and heat—all I could do was press on. Perseverance is not the answer to everything in life, but it is the answer to a lot. I worked to stop the nose bleeds and to watch for combines that were full. There was nothing to do about the dirt and heat and chaff and itching until night. I was slowly discovering that perseverance was my strong suit.

Every night when we did get back to the trailer, I simply had to shower—slimy floor and all. I could never sleep when I was dirty or sweaty or itchy. If I had no access to a shower, all I could think about was feeling miserable and I would lie in bed for hours falling asleep from exhaustion at three or four in the morning. And so, "clean foot syndrome" and all, I would shower.

In Dodge City I found an alternative to showering in our slimy metal rectangle. Here, as in most of our prairie-town stops, one of the regular distractions for the younger wheaties and local teens was pool hopping. Pool hopping was the simple activity of waiting for the community pool to close and the workers to go home, and then climbing the fence for a free swim.

This entertainment was popular with us not because we couldn't afford the twenty-five or fifty cents to swim, but because there was an element of risk in climbing the fence and because we usually got home from the field far after the pool had closed. We also came out an hour later feeling really clean for the first time in days.

After work our first night in Dodge City, Dan and I crept up to the park where we had seen the community pool. It was after 10:00 PM and the pool was closed. We hid in the bushes, and looked across the wide lawn to see a full-blown, raging, after-hours party. There were twenty-five or thirty kids in the pool—diving, laughing, wrestling, splashing and making no attempt whatsoever to be quiet or unseen. We jumped up and joined the party. Getting into the pool was a simple matter of climbing on a storage box and over the chain link fence. We swam for maybe a half an hour, leaving when the kids started to drift off. Our conclusion was simply that the authorities of Dodge City did not care about after-hours use of the pool.

Our second night we came to the edge of the park and looked across at the pool to see no one. The place was quiet and dark—a stark contrast to the party of the previous night. With only one night of data, we assumed that our basic conclusion about police apathy held and climbed the fence for our swim. We were anxious being the only ones there, making us more quiet and careful, but we stayed for some time.

I had then, and retain to this day, a gift for bad timing. Just one minute before we were going to climb out and head back to the trailer, a set of lights came down the road and turned into the pool parking lot. Dan and I were both in the pool and ducked our heads down below the ledge so that we could not be seen. My heart pounded as I gripped the gutter of the pool with my hands and kept the top of my head out to breathe. I had, and retain to this day, a morbid fear of small places like jail cells and was convinced that I was heading to one tonight.

Within moments of hitting the pool, the headlights turned off and a spotlight turned on. For the first minute it swept back and forth across the pool and just above our heads as if the officer was looking carefully for someone. Then it stopped in the dead center of the pool right above our heads and stayed there. I could hear the motor of the patrol car running and was certain that a flashlight-toting officer would be standing above us at any second. I was certain of that for the next twenty minutes as nothing changed. Dan and I gripped the gutter and worried, breathing with our heads tilted back. We whispered about what might happen and about what we should do.

"We can't run! We'll just have to talk to him," I concluded.

Dan whispered back, "He will not care what we have to say! Listen, if he comes up we both just climb the fence and get out like we are going to cooperate. As soon as we get out you run toward the highway and I'll run toward the school. We can both outrun him and we will meet back at the trailer."

"I'm not running!" I said, "We are really in trouble if we get caught. Maybe we can just talk our way out of it and promise not to do it again."

"Fat chance of that!" Dan whispered immediately and said again, "You do what you want to do but I'm running."

So there was our plan—Dan was going to run and I was going to talk. He was a runner by skill and temperament and I was a talker by skill and temperament.

The patrol car motor ran. I was starting to get cold. The spotlight never moved. Five more minutes. Finally, the spotlight went off, the headlights went on, and the car backed out and drove away. Two very cold and anxious wheaties cleared the fence and sprinted for our rented aluminum home.

Much later I realized that the officer was probably entertaining himself by leaving us pinned down there while he read a book. He was simply teaching us a lesson. When he got back to the station he probably said to the dispatcher, "I just iced down a couple of wheaties in the pool for twenty minutes." They both chuckled and knew we would not be in their pool again. It was a joke to them, a nuisance to Dan, and a terror to me.

In Dodge City, I experienced my first truck accident of the summer. It was not a serious wreck, but it was frightening to a sheltered boy who had only been in one auto "accident" in his life.

That previous "accident" involved me and six or eight neighbor kids sitting in the back of our station wagon eating ice cream cones when my Mom backed into a telephone pole. The rear bumper was severely crimped, and one kid lost his ice cream onto the inside of the back window. My Dad never got the bumper fixed, razzed Mom about it mercilessly, and the incident became part of our family lore. "Remember the time Mom put that kid's ice cream on the back window?" was how it usually started. "We don't have to talk about that again!" was how it usually ended. I thankfully had little experience with car wrecks.

Two or three days after our swimming pool problem I was coming back from town with an empty bed and turning off the pavement onto a gravel road. I signaled for a left turn. The road was clear ahead of me—no one coming at all—and there was a pickup behind me. I began to turn. At the same time I turned left, the kid in the pickup decided to pass me. I turned into the left lane. He accelerated into the left lane. We met in the left lane, me nearly broadside to him. There was a terrific jolt and a horrible noise of tearing metal as the hood of his pickup was mashed under the mainframe of my truck. We both came to rest in the ditch next to the gravel road—both upright and welded together by the force of the front end of his pickup under the middle end of my truck.

It was over quickly, and neither of us was close to being hurt. My immediate thoughts turned to Don's reaction and fearing that he was going to kill me. I jumped out of the truck, the driver's door of the other pickup only five feet from me as his pickup was wedged under the truck bed at almost a ninety degree angle. I asked the kid if he was okay. Thankfully, he was fine other than saying, "My dad is going to kill me!" I called Don on the radio and told him what had happened. He was not far away. The kid in the truck had no way to call his dad, so he just stood there with me waiting for something to happen. I asked if he saw my signal and he said he hadn't. I was certain I had signaled but, given my incurable habit of self-guilt, I later decided that I must not have signaled and that it was my fault.

The boy was a little younger than me, maybe 14, and almost identical to me. He may have had a farm driver's license or may have been driving without a license. This was an accident in which no one thought of looking at driver's licenses or insurance papers—which were not be found—or calling the police. It was a "Damn it I wish that hadn't happened!" accident in which everyone drives away annoyed.

He was tall like me and apologetic like me and anxious like me. It would probably be hard to find two more compliant, apologetic, and anxious kids to run into each other in the whole state of Kansas.

Don showed up in only a few minutes and assessed the damage and began to intimidate the kid severely. "Didn't you see that my driver had his signal on?" he asked without even asking me if I had my signal on. "Don't you know not to pass when someone is turning? What the hell were you thinking!?"

Don quickly intimidated the frightened kid into saying it was his fault and then forgave him just as quickly. If the kid's father had come instead of Don the outcome would probably have been just the opposite. I would have been bullied into saying I was wrong and then been forgiven and lectured about safe driving.

As soon as Don had that admission, he jumped in the boy's pickup, started it and backed it furiously out from under my truck. The back tires of the pickup were spitting rock everywhere and there was another horrible metal-on-metal scream. It took some power to get the two rigs free of each other. Though the hood looked horrible the motor was apparently not hurt. There was no damage to my truck other than some red paint ground into the underside of the frame.

Don quickly sent me on my way back to the field and sent the kid on his way back to his dad. It was a case of my advocate arriving before the kid's advocate. I was glad that Don was there intimidating the kid rather than the kid's dad there intimidating me. Events can have starkly different outcomes depending on who arrives at the scene first.

On our first Sunday morning in Dodge City, we were milling around the trucks waiting for Don to do something. We were late getting to the field, and across the street the worship service had started at a Baptist church. I was not a Baptist but I was the only church-going kid or man of any stripe on the crew, thereby giving our crew a very high percentage of churchgoers for a harvest crew.

We seldom knew what day it was, other than it was a cutting day, but we could hear singing and see the lot full of cars—it had to be Sunday. For reasons that are not clear to me—maybe insecurity or rebellion or arrogance or boredom—the singing from inside the church set off a great deal of scoffing and mocking among the crew. I sat on the grass by my truck, my usual anxious self about this irreverence.

Gary was incited by the scoffing to go to his Camaro and put in one of his favorite 8-tracks, "In-A-Gadda-Da-Vida" by Iron Butterfly. He cranked it up until the speakers sounded tinny. Iron Butterfly was in a singing competition with the Dodge City Baptists.

"In-A-Gadda-Da-Vida" had just been released the previous year and covered the entire side of an album. The original title of the song and album were "In the Garden of Eden," but the band members were so drunk and high when they recorded it that they slurred the title. The nonsensical title stuck. The song consisted of two choruses that were both sung three times—the other seventeen minutes was pure instrumental rock.

Thinking that the word "gadda" was a perversion of the name "God," Gary cranked it up more. The word "gadda" was actually a slurred version of the word "garden," but this subtlety was lost on Gary who gloried in the opportunity to make a statement about the foolishness of church-going, God-fearing, hymn-singing and wasting Sunday mornings. After all, one could be out cutting wheat! Wouldn't that be more fun?

"In-A-Gadda-Da-Vida, baby, / don't you know that I'm lovin' you?" Or, as originally written, "In the Garden of Eden, baby, / don't you know that I'm lovin' you?" So, according to Iron Butterfly, in the Garden of Eden Adam was singing to Eve. Neither I nor Gary nor the Baptists got it that morning. The Baptists couldn't hear Gary's serenade, and Gary didn't know that Iron Butterfly was singing a Bible story. There were hymns inside the church about the Bible and rock music outside the church about the Bible, and I took anxious ownership for the whole non-event.

The next day we moved to a new field only a half mile down the road. Don had me move one of the combines. By now, I had driven the combines in the field many times. I had gotten the hang of it—mostly.

I was not particularly good at adjusting the header up and down or at finding the best speed, but I could generally keep the combine on the right track to cut the maximum swath and make the turns in a respectable way. Occasionally I went too wide and missed some wheat and let the guy behind me pick it up. However, in a field of a hundred or more acres, there was not too much to hit. The other combine drivers were experienced enough to stay out of my way.

This was my first time to move a machine on a road. I took it slow and eased out of the field, onto the road and down the road behind the other combines. *Nothing to this!* I thought, and there really wasn't, at least when driving straight down a level road with no other traffic.

A combine is designed to turn quickly. The rear turning wheels will throw the front around in a hurry in order to make a fairly square cut in standing wheat. The trick, as with all cars and machinery, is to know when to turn and how hard to turn and how long to turn and when to straighten out and perhaps most importantly to know where the "corners" of the machine are—actually, that is a lot of tricks. The "corners" of a combine are much further from a driver than the corners of a car or pickup. Plenty of accidents happen when someone who is used to driving a little car gets into a big car or a truck. The accidents happen because the person does not have a good sense of how wide their corners swing when turned.

The field was off to the right. The gate was fairly wide. I was going a little fast. The three machines ahead of me turned in with ease. They turned in with such ease that I relaxed and cruised on up to the gate.

A combine is designed to turn quickly, but this one did not turn quickly enough. Careful as I thought I was being, I turned a little too late and not quite hard enough. I was making a right hand turn and the left front corner of the header was a lot farther out there in space than I thought it was. The corner of the cutter bar slapped the side of the post, and I crammed in the clutch and the brake and the machine began a giant, exaggerated bobbing—both back and forth and up and down. The combine stopped rather quickly, but the header bobbed up and down three or four times—slapping the post every time. No one saw this mess, so I quickly cranked the wheel harder, popped the clutch and got on into the field.

My accidents were mounting and the cost to Don was also mounting. I got off the machine and examined the header carefully. The header wasn't running, so it was impossible to tell exactly how much damage was done. One pulley was visibly bent, but the belt was still in place and it looked like it would work. It did work— the whole summer. Each time I pulled up next to that combine to unload and saw the wobbling pulley, I thanked it for working. I never told Don.

Two or three days later I was in my mode of constant thinking, sitting in the shade of Old Red, when something came together in my head very clearly. It seemed ridiculous that it had taken me so long. From about five different directions little bits of evidence came together.

At breakfast one day that week I had made a joke about Don always "going for parts." He was gone from the fields a lot, and he generally said he was going for parts or trying to drum up some new wheat to cut. When I made the quip, Don had given me a little scowl and Marie had noticeably stiffened at the stove. I was trying to be funny, but it was clearly not funny and I dropped it immediately. The rest of the crew was tense and quiet. No one picked it up.

After breakfast I had barely cleared the hearing range of the Dexter's trailer when Mark pulled me aside and said, "Don't ever talk about running for parts again! Don't talk about that around Marie or Don if you want to keep your head!"

"I was just making a joke," I protested, "what's wrong with that?" I was feeling defensive and unfairly judged for having done nothing but try to bring a little fun to a fairly somber breakfast table.

"Just take my word for this," was Mark's answer, "and stay away from that subject." Mark didn't say why.

It was not until this moment leaning against a tire that I connected Marie's anger with her suspicion and incessant checking on the whereabouts of her husband. I felt sorry for her. Going for parts was apparently a euphemism for "I have a meeting with someone, someone female."

In my teen naïveté I thought there must be something that could be done to fix it right away—something like putting new belts on a combine or welding a broken truck panel. Apparently, there was nothing that Marie could do, at least nothing that she had yet conceived to do.

She never solved it. We seldom solve other people's behavior.

Don Dexter was an incurable womanizer. He was so addicted that he was hardly working to hide it anymore. Marie couldn't stop him.

She could do other things in response but she couldn't stop him.

One night in Dodge City, Dan and I left the trailer park at after 10:00 PM with the expressed plan of buying a six pack of beer each and drinking it all. It was one of my more diligent pursuits as a teen. I hated the taste of beer and our plan was not hatched because it was something particularly pleasurable to me. Perhaps I felt that drinking a six pack by myself, one can after the other, was somehow a validation of maturing or rebellion or manhood, or maybe a declaration of independence. Maybe it was just the novelty. Maybe it was the risk. My motivations for this plan were not clear to me.

The trick, of course, was going to be getting someone to sell beer to two fresh-faced and obviously underage teens. We contemplated what to say and what lies to tell in tandem. We contemplated whether to plead with the clerk if he or she called our bluff and refused to sell. We rehearsed how to look and what to say and how to act. To our surprise it turned out to be no issue at all.

I followed Dan into the first gas station that was open—a tired and dingy Mom and Pop kind of place with far too much merchandise stuffed in far too little space. We each selected a six pack of Coors 3.2% cans and brought them to the counter attempting to look older—however one does that. We also attempted to look confident and nonchalant—however an obviously underage, first-time beer buyer does that.

The man behind the counter was in his mid-thirties and looked like a wheatie who had gotten tired of the travel. Clearly he was a savvy and worldly-wise man. Clearly, he knew what was happening or at least attempting to happen, but he never batted an eye. He simply took our money, bagged our beer and sent us on our way. We were not carded, questioned or even grinned at. Apparently, what we wanted to pass off as an everyday occurrence—selling beer to minors—was truly an everyday occurrence in that town or at least in that gas station. His interest was not in upholding the laws of the state of Kansas but in putting money in the till. He did put money in the till, we all broke the law, and we all were happy.

We took our individual sacks, left the store and headed for the nearest park. We had seen the park before on our two trips to the pool. It was dark and quiet and off the beaten path—just the place to pull off our dangerous feat.

We continued in our mode of attempted acting. Walk regular. Be casual. Be cool. Act like two guys out on an innocent grocery errand at 10:15 PM—picking up some eggs and milk for breakfast. In this mode, being cool and casual, we walked right past the local police station. This had not been in our plan. Even Dan's heart picked up a few beats as we walked past. There was a light on inside, but we could see no one. Two patrol cars were parked outside, one of which was probably one that we had already encountered at the pool—at least encountered its spotlights. No one saw us and perhaps there was only a dispatcher inside or no one at all.

Two brushes with the law in one town. It turned out that Dodge City was "wicked and dangerous" after all, at least a little and at least for me. We could have been hauled in for pool hopping and underage drinking. Scared as I was, these two charges, even if convicted, would not land us in the Kansas State Penitentiary. I would have been terrified to be in any "police house." What inspired my "lawlessness" is hard to know and it certainly was not respectable as crime sprees go. In the "Wicked Little City" of 100 years ago my escapades would scarcely be a school prank.

A few blocks down from the station was the park with a picnic table in the middle and in the dark. Sitting on top of the table we began our task of drinking six cans of Coors apiece. We talked about the summer and what we liked and didn't like and were hoping for. We talked about how different everything had been from our expectations and what we were going to do when we got home. We talked about Don and of the rest of the crew. We talked about Marie and her sadness. We talked about half wishing we had not taken this job and half being really glad we had.

Dan and I had the most connected conversation of the summer that night on that table with our 3.2% beers and our "getting-away-with-it" adventure. Yet both of us knew we would not be connected back at school. In the common way of life, we were thrown together for a short, intense time and then our lives diverged again. We were both fine with that.

Drinking the six beers was not a difficult task in the scale of world accomplishments. We took it slow and did not get drunk by any real drinker's definition of drunk. We had to pee a lot and overall didn't much enjoy the experience. But we finished the task and congratulated ourselves and even disposed of the cans lawfully in a nearby trash can. We had taken a risk and done something for the first time without getting caught. Mission accomplished.

As we eased to the trailer through the dark, I felt a bit light headed. I felt the slightest loss of control in my balance and walking, but tried not to let Dan see any of that. I had been out of control plenty of times with childhood epilepsy, and those spells had been terrifying to me. Loss of control, to beer or epilepsy or anything else has never been much fun to me.

I relieved myself again, eased down on my cot and closed my eyes. There was a lightness in my brain and a gentle, gyrating motion. The next thing I knew it was morning, and I had to pee real, real bad.

Don was in constant combine repair mode now. Only a few weeks into the summer, the machines were showing their age and succumbing to the wear and tear of long daily use. His parts runs now were clearly more for parts and less for womanizing.

One of the Gleaners threw an entire set of belts one evening and had to be shut down. Don must have seen it plenty of times before and was not upset about it. His only comment was, "There goes another hundred bucks out of my pocket." In the morning he went to the implement dealer and bought the one hundred dollars or so worth of belts. He was soon in the field, sweating and working on the replacement of the destroyed belts while the other machines and trucks operated around him. It was hot, and his shirt was completely wet and sticking to his hairy back and beer belly. His gut hung out below the soaked shirt as he knelt in the stubble and dirt, straining and tightening and adjusting. The work was not fun, but Don went about it in a steady and stoic manner. While he could cuss with the best custom harvester, he was steady and quiet today. Occasionally he would ask me for help with prying a tensioner pulley or tightening a bolt between my runs to the elevator.

When the chore was finally done, he told me to get on the machine and fire her up. I got up on the machine—sitting maybe eight feet above him—and started the engine. "Put the header in gear!" he shouted above the pounding motor. I did that. I sat on the machine with the entire mechanism running while Don looked at the belts and listened to the sound and evaluated the repair. He did not look satisfied but shouted for me to cut one round. I put her in gear, let out the clutch and turned toward the standing wheat. I was heading for a corner so as to start at a place that would not throw off the pattern of the cut.

Though I only drove this particular machine at lunch hours, I still had an ear for how it should sound, and it did not sound right. I contemplated shutting it down but decided that since Don had repaired it, looked at it running, listened to it and sent me on a round that it must be okay.

It was not okay. Something was not tensioned right or the original problem that broke the first set of belts was still present. Before the combine even got to the wheat, there was a horrible snapping sound, flying rubber and shutting down machinery. I smashed in the clutch and the brake, bringing the machine to a bobbing stop. I shut it down and looked back at Don.

This time he was doing some respectable cussing. He was not cussing at me but at the machine and the lost time and the additional hundred bucks.

When Don and I both stood beside the machine looking at the several empty pulleys and the scattered parts of belts, I stupidly admitted, "Something did not sound right to me when I was driving it, Don." Immediately I wished I had not said it.

He must have figured that whatever happened was his fault and not mine. To his credit, many a foreman would have taken the opportunity to vent his spleen on me even if he knew full well it was his fault. Don did not.

All he said was, "I wish you had shut her down."

"I'm sorry," I said.

Don turned and walked off to his pickup.

The next set of belts worked, and worked fine. I marveled again at watching this determined man kneeling in the dust and straw and heat while installing a set of belts that he had just installed that morning. He was simply doing what needed to be done—unpleasant and difficult as it was. In these settings Don was steady and determined: a genuine finisher. He did not seem to feel that life had given him a raw deal for the loss of two sets of belts in twelve hours. He adjusted to the reality of it all and fixed it. I gave away too much emotional energy nurturing the feelings that life had given me a raw deal at one juncture or another. Don's approach to the "double belt day" helped me to see that much of life is adjusting to what is real and steadily getting it done.

Don Dexter, like all of us, was a person of commendable good and deplorable bad. He could be diligent, kind, forgiving, hardworking, patient and occasionally even generous. The other side of him ignored his wife and children and was deeply committed to his personal wealth. Don applied his admirable diligence and work ethic primarily to making money and finding agreeable women.

Don wore sweat-soaked shirts with tired embroidery that read: "Don Dexter Custom Harvesting." The shirts had been made in a time when Don was much more conscious of the image and marketing of his company. Now they were threadbare, and he wore them because he had lots of them. He put them on as a matter of habit and, like all of us, did not give thought to something that was very familiar to him. He was too close to the shirts and the routine to see that the shirts now projected the image of a business that was staggering, tired and unconcerned with what others thought.

Don chewed tobacco, smoked when he wasn't chewing, was given to slouching and walked with a lazy shuffling in his worn out, round-toed field boots—perhaps due to the worn out feeling of his body and his soul. His face was not particularly attractive and his cheeks were puffy. His hair was brown and unruly. He habitually focused on making money more than on personal appearance and fitness, and certainly more than on his marriage and three kids.

One evening in Dodge City, Marie and the kids were gone for a couple of days. Don "dressed up" with the explicit purpose of walking down a few trailers and propositioning the wife of a fellow harvester who was gone. He showered and put on a clean shirt and let all of us know what he was up to. "Wish me luck," he said as he left the trailer. Why he would announce this was unclear to me. Perhaps he was confident of a "conquest" and was making a statement like Babe Ruth pointing his bat to the fence and promising a home run.

As he walked out the door, I watched him in his "cleaned up and dressed up" mode and thought to myself, "Why would any woman, even if she was immoral and without inhibitions, be interested in this man—big gut hanging out from under his shirt, hint of tobacco juice on the corner of his mouth, three days stubble of beard, horrible haircut, crooked teeth, dirty pants and not a particularly attractive face."

Either the woman had integrity or she saw Don exactly as I saw him or both. Don came home disappointed.

On our last day in Dodge City I was unloading on the go and quite comfortable now with the process. I had become experienced enough to keep track of the various pieces of the process that I controlled. I could speed up and slow down to spread out the pile of the stream of wheat and then pull slightly and slowly off to the left, away from the lumbering combine, when the hopper was empty and the auger was shut off. Then, once clear of the combine, I would simply let off the gas, let the truck bog down and get inside to drive to my waiting spot or, if I was full, drive to my granary or elevator and unload.

By now I had done this a lot and had really had no trouble other than spilling a small amount of wheat. But today, for the only time that summer, there was some object in my way. It was where there should have been no object—in the middle of a wheat field in the stubble where a combine had already cut. The object was a single rock a little smaller than a basketball. How it got there and how it was still there when the combine has already passed is mysterious. The rest of the field was clean of rocks and very flat.

But the rock was there, and I hit it with a glancing blow with the left side of my front left tire. It hit the left side of my steering tire, throwing the entire truck to the right. The blow happened so fast and I was not prepared for it. The steering wheel was jerked out of my hands, and the truck took a sharp, if temporary, right turn. The sharp turn threw the front fender of my old Ford into the side of the combine header.

I jerked immediately away. Kerry was driving the combine, and he had not been watching me. He jerked his head over with a scowl and shouted, "What the hell did you do!?" I knew he shouted that because I read his lips. I couldn't hear anything of what he said over the din of the running combine.

As soon as he shut off the auger, I pulled away and he stopped the machine leaving it running. We both got out to inspect the damage. There was barely a scratch on the fender of Old Red. No harm done there. On the side of the header there was one pulley that was slightly bent. The header was still running and running fine though with a distinct wobble in that one pulley. The belt seemed to be operating fine and in no danger of coming off. Outside of that there was no obvious damage.

I told Kerry what had happened over the noise of the machine and even pointed out the rock. He shook his head in disgust and crawled back on the machine.

I didn't say anything to Don. I hoped Kerry wouldn't say anything to Don, and that the pulley would work. It did work. It worked the whole summer. Each time I eased up next to that combine to take his wheat and saw the wobbling pulley, I thanked it for working. Now, half way through the summer, two of the four combines now had bent header pulleys because of my handiwork.

Our wheat ran out in Dodge City. More wheat was ripening north of us. Combines had to be unhooked from their headers and loaded on the trucks. We hit the field early in the morning—as we did on most moving days. There was no moisture content to worry about today—only the moving of tons of metal. I fought the boxes off Old Red with my crowbar. By now I was familiar with which panels stuck and how to get them unstuck. Life is so much easier when you know the systems and the quirks. Once the panels were off and piled in the stubble, I pulled the truck out on the road, backed it into the ditch, and rammed the bed against the dirt on the other side. Shortly Don was along with a combine and eased it up onto the bed.

Once the combine was in place, it was my job to chain it down with the chains and tensioners. I would hook one end of the chain on the tie-down bar on one side of the bed, run the chain up over the axle of the combine, and put the other hook in place on the tie-down bar on the other side of the bed. Next was the tensioner, which was a short chunk of chain with hooks at each end and a handle in the middle that worked a pulley system to pull the tie-down chain tight. The trick was to hook the tensioner chain hooks at the right place on the tie-down chain in order to put terrific tension on the chain but still be able to break the handle over and lock it in place. If you hooked too short, you could not break the handle over. If you hooked too long, there would not be enough tension on the chain to hold the combine securely.

The handle of the tensioner had to be pulled over using a "cheater pipe." It was simply a steel pipe that was big enough to slip all the way over the handle of the tensioner and long enough to get some leverage on the handle. It would be impossible to get the chain tight enough with the tensioner's own handle—we simply did not have the leverage or the strength. If the chain tension was right, the tires on the combine would be slightly squashed and the four tons of metal would be as secure to the bed as it needed to be—under regular driving conditions. For a combine to slip in this piggy-back situation was big trouble. The trouble could be as big as torn up machinery or death.

Once I had all my combine chains in place, I stacked the box panels under the combine and chained them in place using chains and tensioners, though without any need for the same kinds of tension that held the combine to the bed. Then I would pull up out of the ditch in the lowest gear—"granny gear"—and back up to my header trailer. The trailer was hooked on the ball, locked on the ball, connected with break-away chains and connected to the wiring collar so that the lights on the truck and the lights on the trailer both did the same thing at the same time—in theory.

Along the edge of the field, this same process was happening with three other combines, trucks, headers, box panels, chains and header trailers. It was a flurry of activity that would have looked crazy in time-lapse photography. Each driver and helper not only worked on his own truck, but helped when some problem arose on another truck. The cheater pipes were handed back and forth between drivers. Trailers were jockeyed into place. Mechanically-savvy guys fussed with malfunctioning wiring. Trucks that would not come out of the loading ditch were hooked and pulled. Headers were chained to their trailers.

Tire pressures were checked and filled from the compressor on the service truck. Steadily the completely loaded trucks were eased out onto the gravel road and lined up in whatever order they were completed.

When my loading was finished, I pulled in line behind two finished trucks and walked back to see what could be done to help with the remaining truck. I felt a sense of accomplishment in finishing the load and a sense of surprise at how much I had learned in a few weeks. I was now doing tasks with ease that a few weeks ago I had never even heard of, let alone done. It felt surprisingly good to me.

Immersion is a great learning method for language acquisition and for wheat harvesting and for many skills. I was "thrown in the deep end" of custom harvesting—at least in my little corner of the pool. The first time someone was there watching to tell me that I did not have enough tension on my tie-down chains. The rest of the time I was there alone to figure out where the tensioner hooks go to get the right tension and keep an expensive machine secured to another expensive machine. The feeling of some level of skill and expertise felt great to me that day. I had no idea how to fix a combine or get a new customer. But I knew my small part of the game and I was getting it done.

The events of the summer continued to imprint on me—the people, the happenings, the scenery, the near-misses, the difficulties, the new chores—all of it. They imprinted very powerfully on me for many reasons.

For one thing, I never thought about what time it was or whether I was allowed to go out at night or when I had to be back. On this summer adventure it never occurred to me to tell someone I was going somewhere. I never had to defend or detail who I was going with or had actually been with. In a couple of months I would be asking to go out and, if allowed to go, would be required to tell where I was going and who I was going with and when I would be back. In Dodge City or Alva or Ness City I could get off work and go wherever I wanted and tell no one and come back whenever I wanted and never be asked who I was with or what I did. This was my first serious taste of freedom and it was about the best thing I had ever eaten.

The summer also imprinted me because I had to act responsibly for probably the first time in my life. I had to go to work and perform at work and do my own laundry. At home my laundry magically moved from the corner of my room, where I had thrown it in a smelly pile, to my drawer—clean, folded and smelling wonderful. Now I had to get off work, shower, gather my dirty clothes, get a pocket full of quarters, walk to the laundromat, and do my own laundry. My first time there I had to ask for help about how much soap to put in and how much clothes a washer would take. The woman tried to explain to me about colors and whites but after that first time I didn't much trouble myself with sorting. I would not fold my clothes but they did come back clean—stuffed inside the same bag in which they came to the laundromat.

A third reason for the remarkable impact on me was that I had a real job. I had to get up and go to work and do something helpful and I was getting paid for it, or at least I was assured that I would get paid for it. I had worked part-time during the school year or full-time in the summers since I was in sixth grade. I had been a windshield washer, a potato peeler, a babysitter, a fry cook, a lawn mower, a paperboy, and a car washer. But now I had a big boy job with a driver's license and the use of a big truck. I had the potential to really help things or really hurt things. This was a much bigger deal than getting the paper on the correct front porch.

Additionally, I remember so much because there were so many "firsts" for me in this summer. The list is long. Just to mention one, it was the first time I was almost dismembered. A wheat auger is not a friendly piece of metal. When you should have lost your hand or your arm but did not, the memory is indelible.

Finally, I thought I knew a lot about people and how they acted. But I knew next to nothing in the vast ocean of human behavior and relational function or dysfunction. I knew the people in my own family very well and I had some inkling of the "dance" we did together—some functional and some dysfunctional. But I had no clue about the larger world of human actions and motivations and relationships. Don's dishonesty impressed me. Marie's anger impressed me. The sad dance between the two of them impressed me. The Three Musketeers' irresponsibility impressed me. Cliff's skills as a loner impressed me. Mark's aloofness impressed me.

The summer experience was even more radically different from home than I had imagined it would be. I am a person with a horrible memory but I would remember this wheatie summer so vividly and so long that it shocked me.

6 NESS CITY, KANSAS

*It was one of the many troubles in life
into which I poured mounds of anxiety and
which turned out to be a non-event.*

We rolled into Ness City, Kansas, where Don had cut for years, with our patched-up metal parade. Ness City, like many of the towns we rolled into, might more appropriately be called "Nesstown" or "Nessberg" or "Ness Hamlet" or "Ness Village" or "Ness Wide Spot in the Road." But Ness Wide Spot in The Road, Kansas, is hard to market. In fairness to Ness City, with a population of maybe two thousand people, it was certainly bigger than many of the burgs where we landed.

Ness City's claim to fame was the four-story Old Ness County Bank Building. Nicknamed the "Skyscraper of the Plains," she sits in the middle of the town. The stone monolithic rectangle was finished in 1890 and was a source of terrific pride for decades in Ness City. However, the intervening eight decades had not been kind to her. To a sixteen-year-old wheatie she looked simply old, tired, and ugly. I looked at her the way a teenager looks at an elderly person and insanely believes that the person did something wrong to have gotten old and haggard—then adds to the insanity by believing that they themselves will not be subject to the fate of aging.

The money and effort that went into the Old Ness County Bank Building had to be substantial. We love what we invest in, and someone or many "someones" certainly loved that building. We all value our own things. And we naturally devalue the things that we did not invest in.

In Ness City we began our usual routine of parking the trailers, deciding which wheat to cut first, and looking for more acres. By now we knew this routine well and worked it well, but it had plenty of challenges. Headers wouldn't attach right and had to be jockeyed repeatedly—one guy on each end fighting to align the bolts, hooks, holes and pins while the driver tried to raise and lower the connector hoping to find the right alignment. First the header was too high and then too low and tempers flared. Words were exchanged. Jockeying continued. Victory at last. Combines came perilously close to coming off the truck beds. Trailer parks that were open last year were slammed full this year. Farmers who used Dexter Custom Harvesting last year had bought their own combine for this year, or were late planting and their wheat was not ready. Farmers who needed a harvester were talking to two or three other guys.

We did all this for seventy-five cents an hour since the combines were not running. My ongoing anxiety throughout the summer was the question of Don's records about how much I had worked and therefore about how much he owed me. I had not been keeping track of my hours, and Mark chastised me for it. He assured me that Dexter would screw me if I did not have a pretty good idea of the actual hours I had worked for him. By now I figured it was too late to start. The sane route would have been to forget it and take what worked out. Instead, I chose my usual route which was to dwell on it, worry and pour emotional energy into a black hole, and nothing at all changed in what was going to be written on my end-of-summer paycheck.

In Ness City we encountered, for the second time, a custom harvest crew that was notorious for reckless driving in wheat trucks. On their trips from the field to the elevator and back to the field, they drove crazy fast. The crazy fast was not about high productivity, but testosterone. The risks of driving crazy fast clearly did not fit into any sane business plan for a custom harvester. They might have moved a little more wheat, but they were certainly inviting something tragic that would cost far more than a few extra loads over the course of a summer. These drivers compounded each other's craziness with boasting, challenges and competitions. "I got to town and back in forty-eight minutes!" was the daytime equivalent of the nighttime command, "Hold my beer and watch this." In either case the outcome was not going to be good.

They drove five brand new, cab-over, purple Fords. They were beautiful, matching trucks—easily the nicest trucks of any custom crew we encountered. Most custom harvesters had a menagerie of machinery just like Don Dexter Custom Harvesting. It was rare for a harvester to have matching trucks and even more rare to have new trucks. With the cab-over design the nose was very short, and the driver sat much higher than in a regular truck, making the drivers look like a kings looking down on the regular folks. There is something beautiful about a new, powerful, well-designed machine, and these purple Fords had it. As I lumbered around in my Ford—the oldest in Don's fleet and the roughest—I was covetous of those trucks. No one was coveting our trucks.

In Ness City, as in all the stops, our work hours were unpredictable. Most nights we cut late—as long as the moisture content allowed. When we did stop, we were generally too tired for the routine of maintenance on the machines. Most mornings started with that routine which seemed to go much better in the daylight anyway. Belts were checked and every zerk on every vehicle was greased—or was supposed to be greased. Each man was responsible for his own combine or his own truck. As a truck driver I had far less maintenance than the combine guys. When they finished the combines quickly, everyone knew they had done the "speed lube" and left a few zerks for tomorrow.

Many days on the custom crew were more boredom for me as a truck driver than hard work. I sat next to my truck and zoned out in a pattern of waiting and driving, loading and unloading. One of the results of this pattern was a major deterioration in my physical fitness from the spring track season until Ness City. This pattern would continue from Ness City until football season, and I would regret it mightily. The work had periods of exertion to be sure, but very little aerobic exercise and very little to keep the pounds from gathering around my gut as I ate greasy-spoon food, farm food and fast food, and plenty of it.

The major variety in this pattern of loading, unloading and waiting was the length of lines at the elevator. On good days I would be the only truck. I weighed in with my load, dumped my wheat and weighed out empty. On the bad days I sat in a long line of trucks, dust blowing and sweat running down my back, as I inched up to unload. Tempers could run high in the hot afternoon lines. I kept to myself for the most part and didn't let any gap form between me and the truck ahead of me. Bullies cutting in line were not uncommon—just like at the water fountain in third grade. I was always happy to get my weight slip, stuff it in the glove box envelope, and leave.

The mechanized elevator was first invented and constructed in Buffalo, New York, in 1843 and was used for unloading grain from ships onto canal barges. For the first time in history, grain was handled in bulk rather than in individual sacks that had to be manually unloaded and reloaded. The mechanical elevator revolutionized the handling of wheat—increasing the efficiency of handling many fold.

Obviously, elevator owners make money by buying wheat at a lower price than they sell it for. They buy from the farmer, store it and sell later when the prices are more favorable or when a pre-arranged contract with an end user kicks in. Early on in America most farmers realistically had only one elevator where they could store their grain. Other elevators were simply too far away from their fields to feasibly transport their grain. The result was that the local elevator had a monopoly on storage for their little area and could pay lower than market prices simply because the farmer had no choice.

However, for one of the countless times in world history David beat Goliath. This miniature-monopoly practice was broken up in two ways. First, many governments began to regulate wheat prices and prohibit individual elevators from setting basement prices. Second, many farmers began banding together in large "cooperatives" and buying their local elevator or building a new one so that they could cooperate together and assure that they got the best possible prices for themselves. In effect, they gave the best possible price for wheat because they were buying from themselves and selling for themselves. These elevators became known as "Co-ops," and they exist all over the wheat regions of North America.

My most frightening incident at an elevator happened in Ness City. It was not caused by the aggression of one of the drivers but by the habit of one of the drivers. For a couple of days at the height of the local harvest here the lines at our elevator were long and slow. I was inching forward behind a newish Chevy and keeping to myself, as was my habit. Somehow I had developed a cue in the presence of other harvest crews to keep my head low and do my work and move on back to the comfort of our own crew. I did it all summer long, on cue.

I was only two trucks from the dump chute when the driver in the newish Chevy ahead of me acted on one of the habitual cues in his life—he lit a cigarette. He felt a little piece of boredom or tiredness or aggression or anxiety or hunger or some physical twitch or some emotional longing and did what he always did on that cue—he lit up. He was only a truck-length from entering the elevator.

When the truck ahead of him moved on Mr. Chevy eased up into the elevator. I eased out on the clutch of Old Red and moved closer so I would be ready next. As I was easing forward, only ten feet behind the Chevy, a violent scream of profanity streamed and a succession of related words streamed out of the elevator operator's booth. The tone of the voice was angry but far more than that it was terrified. It was exactly what and how a man would scream if he were falling down a pit to his death. No exaggeration. It was the voice of terror.

I didn't smoke and I didn't pay any attention to the signs either. What I did not know is that wheat dust is highly volatile and will explode with a ferocity that is almost always deadly. Years and years of wheat—moved in and moved out—left wheat dust that, when mixed with oxygen and a spark, caused horrible explosions, fires, loss of life and loss of property. Any truck driver smoking anywhere near the elevator would hopefully catch hell before he caused hell.

The elevator operator, seeing a driver smoking in his open cab inside the elevator, was very sure that hell was coming immediately.

The operator must have run out the office door to the outside and saved his own life. The driver must have put the cigarette out inside the cab—I didn't see him throw it. If he had thrown it I am not sure what the injury would have been to him or me or the several other people and drivers nearby.

When the crisis was over the operator came back and began with an adrenaline-driven tirade against the driver. I sat leaning out the window of my truck watching the tongue lashing.

The men were only a couple of feet apart. The operator kept shouting and deriding. The sheepish driver was rapidly transitioning from sheepish to perfectly angry himself. Timid as I was I got out of my truck and eased closer. I was either going to stop a fight or see a fight. Before I got five feet away one of the other elevator operators came between the men. He didn't even say anything but his presence seemed to break the trance and sent his still-shaking coworker out of the building. I had just witnessed two near explosions averted in two minutes. The calmer operator processed Mr. Chevy and we all moved on.

I had seen the numerous and obvious "Absolutely No Smoking" signs on the elevators everywhere and all summer long. Unfortunately, so had Mr. Chevy and these signs had become too common for him to notice any longer. His cue to light up over-shadowed his conscious knowledge that it was both suicidal and homicidal.

The very next afternoon I was lost in the zone of heat and boredom and mindlessly creeping forward with the long line of waiting trucks. For some reason on this day I was extra anxious to dump and get out of there. The line crept forward. It was the elevator version of rush hour complete with no rushing involved. My patience waned. Finally I reached the scale, reached the dump floor, stood on my running board and pulled the lever of the dump bed, and felt the by now routine feel of the rising truck as the avalanche of wheat disappeared into the floor. As soon as my bed was down, I pulled out, turned onto the highway and headed for the field. The full combines would be waiting for me back at the field—the long lines meant combines were cutting faster than trucks were hauling. Some machines might even be parked waiting to be unloaded.

Half way back to the field, Gary flagged me down as he was heading for the elevator. He was very serious which was unusual for him and also very condescending which was normal for him. He informed me that I had forgotten to weigh after I dumped the load and that Don was furious. The elevator had radioed Don about my mistake. My timid heart immediately raced. Gary assured me that Don was going to kick my ass from here to Canada and that I had screwed up in a major way.

For the next few miles and few minutes, my heart kept racing as I anticipated being chewed out and ridiculed by Don—I had, even back then, a gift for anticipating the worst.

When I got back to the field Don pulled his pickup to a stop, leaned out the window, grinned, and said, "Whaddya do that for?" He was not at all angry—only amused and happy to have something on me that he could bring up regularly.

"I'm sorry," I basically stammered. I was somewhere in the Bermuda Triangle between relieved and surprised and still scared. "I was in such a long line that when I finally got out of there I just forgot."

"Well tomorrow you can go and get it weighed. No big deal," he responded and drove off. I felt like a new driver who had experienced his first traffic stop and only to be informed that his tail light was burned out.

The first thing the next day, even though we hadn't cut anything yet, Don sent me to town with my empty truck to be weighed and another conjured up errand of some kind. I got my precious weight slip and put it in the envelope.

It was one of the many troubles in life into which I poured mounds of anxiety and which turned out to be a non-event. Part of the anxiety had been caused by Gary with his words of dire warning about Don's anger. Either Don had cooled down or, more likely, Gary was jacking with me. He saw me as a timid and impressionable kid who could be jerked around and spun up. His read on me was accurate.

The whole crew moved to a new field that afternoon and I now had a new, and much longer, route to town. The road from the field to the highway was fairly straight but full of small rises and falls—like a gentle roller coaster. As I descended into one trough, I could not see above the crest of the hill ahead of me. It was like riding a small boat in ocean swells. For a moment I was in a trough and could not see anything. The next moment I was on the crest and could see everything.

The ride into town on this roller coaster was far different than the ride coming out of town. Going in loaded was plenty fun and even more fun when I pushed the speed up a little. The ride coming out empty was bone jarring and even more so when I pushed the speed up a little.

Going in fully loaded Old Red felt like a huge, heavy, old Cadillac with very bad shocks—much like floating on the ocean in swells. She would not accelerate for anything. I could mash the bare metal accelerator to the bare metal floor board and hear the whine of the engine go higher, but not feel any acceleration. It was an exercise in patience to wait for some speed. It was also a fight to stop my loaded truck. The first time I tried to stop when it was loaded was an education. Good brakes or not, several tons of metal and wheat have a momentum that is not easily arrested. The job is only done with braking and downshifting together.

I had already learned that this loaded truck did not respond quickly to a quick jerk of the wheel. Jerking the front end away from a rock or dog would likely result in hitting the object and maybe rolling.

But most of all the feel of a loaded wheat truck is that of gentle lumbering and swaying. As a driver you can feel the weight through your back, butt and hands. You know when the physics of the truck have changed dramatically. You are attached to something so much more powerful and massive than yourself that you have immediate respect for the sheer mass and power of the thing. It is true that you have a steering wheel, an accelerator and a brake, but those have limited power in the face of the great mass of the load. You can speed up but not very quickly. You can stop but only with great effort and plenty of distance. You can turn but not sharply.

When cresting a rise in the road, the whole load and truck keep going up for a split second and then settle down again as the shocks and springs are overloaded and mashed beyond their capacity and rebound. When taking a corner, the truck and load want to go out in the ditch and everything strains to stay on the road—sometimes even with straining it follows the direction that the mass was going before the driver turned the wheel.

Coming back to the field empty was rough and harsh—both as the truck responded to the troughs and crests and as she responded to the very surface of the dirt road. An empty wheat truck, while no BMW, is more responsive to acceleration, braking and turning. It is also a lot rougher to ride in. With no weight on the shocks and springs, every pothole, rock and stretch of washboard is kidney-jarring.

I enjoyed the coaster-like hills in the loaded Ford as I went from field to elevator. It was a strange combination of gentle up and down floating, with the near-fear of the mass that was making you float and was two feet behind your body.

Returning from the elevator shortly after we moved to this roller coaster road, I had my second accident. I didn't feel that I was at fault in either one—though a more experienced driver might have avoided both.

Wheat trucks have huge mirrors. They stick far out from the cab so that the driver can see around the wheat box or around a combine tire when a combine has been chained on the bed. They are also tall—between twelve and eighteen inches high and eight or so inches wide. An already wide truck becomes wider with two mirrors sticking out to the side like massive, hideous glass ears.

I was climbing out of a swale, going too fast, and could not see over the crest of the hill in front of me. I was on my side of the road though the road was not wide—especially when two wheat trucks passed each other. As I crested the hill, another wheat truck was right there—too far on my side of the road, going much too fast and only visible to me at the last moment. Instinctively, in the split second available to me, I jerked the front of my Ford to the right as much as I dared without shooting into the ditch and risking a rollover. The guy in the other cab was a teenager like me—my brain registered and still retains the look of fear on his face in that instant when we were right on each other. He may still remember the look of fear on my face.

From all I could tell he made no correction at all. Either he panicked and couldn't do anything, or he figured it was up to me to move or he knew that any correction in a loaded truck would be disaster. He never changed his course.

Between the moment when we saw each other and the time we met each other were a few short seconds. It was not near enough time to make much correction with two-ton trucks. As we passed each other, the back of his mirror mashed into the back of my mirror. The impact of mirror on mirror sent tiny triangles of mirror shrapnel through my open window. It sprayed my face, hands, arms, chest and neck.

The cabs of the two trucks and the beds of the two trucks missed each other by inches. In that flashing instant when the two trucks passed, my brain, via my side vision, registered a flash of purple and the box of his truck being inches from the side of my head and even fewer inches from my truck.

The shattering glass shot-gunning into my face especially heightened the shock and fear. Adrenaline spiked in my system. My heart rate exploded. My brain registered that I was going to die.

In one moment I was sure I was going to die. In the next moment I realized that I was not going to die and that I was not really even hurt. I had two or three small nicks from the sailing mirror fragments on the left side of my face and neck—they barely bled.

My heart had gone from sixty beats per minute up to two hundred beats per minute in about five seconds. The result was severe trembling and an inability to think. I got on my brakes and brought my truck to a stop well off the side of the road in the right side ditch. Sitting there in the cab I continued to shake, and my heart was pounding with a force that in itself scared me. After some time, my mind began to emerge from the fog of fear, and I stepped down from the cab on the dirt road and on shaky legs. Looking back into the cab, I saw the miniature triangles of mirror on the seat, floor and even the dash. It was hard to believe that an eight-by-eighteen inch mirror could make that many little triangles.

My mind had just begun to rehearse what I was going to say to the other driver when I realized that he had not stopped. He was gone. He was gone to town with his load and his mangled mirror and I would never see him again. He knew he was in the middle of the road and going too fast, and he did not want to discuss that with anyone.

I imagine that he told his boss, "Some kid in an old Ford was in the middle of the road and going too fast and I barely got out of his way when we both hit the top of the hill." He probably also had some choice words for me and my horrible driving. He probably got a new mirror for his beautiful purple truck. I used my right hand mirror until I found an old mirror to tape on the mirrorless bracket of my truck. The replacement mirror did not fit at all—it was too big and the wrong shape. But it did succumb to some serious taping. I viewed this makeshift beauty as another piece of my summer legacy of torn up equipment.

Don took it all in stride. He said he was glad I was not hurt and went about his day. He had other things on his mind—broken machines or getting some more acres to cut or the woman he met in the parts house that morning, or all three.

The next day it rained—one of the worst things that can happen right at harvest time. The grain was too wet to cut, and the driveways into the fields were too wet to try. While we waited for it to stop, we greased every zerk that Don Dexter owned, checked and tightened every belt and swapped tires here and there. When that was all done, some make-work projects cropped up in and around the trailers. The work was easy but boring. Our morale was in the ditch because we were not making any money and we all knew we were being kept busy for the sake of busy.

When the wheat finally dried enough to cut, we went at it with a vengeance. We were behind on the Ness City wheat and needed to get to the wheat that was ripening up in North Platte, Nebraska. These two days set off a domino effect all up the line. The biggest worry in all this was that we would not show up in a given field when we said we would be there and an impatient farmer would hire one of the other crews that were grubbing around for work.

Our first day back in the field was a mess. The roads were like snot, and every run was full of anxiety about getting stuck or sliding into a gate. I would get up some momentum while I still had some traction in the stubble field and then guide the front of the truck along the slippery mud—with the marginal control that I had—and up on to the road. The operation had the general feel of driving a jeep on ice—you might get some traction, but steering was sketchy. Once the rig was going a direction, I had little or no traction to change that direction.

About mid-morning Mark did get a truck stuck. As he came out of the field, he was going too slow to cross a huge mud trap. He could have cleared it easily with some speed. When he realized his mistake, he tried to double clutch and downshift so he could goose it. He missed the double clutch timing, and the truck would not go into the lower gear. It slowed, slowed more as he was fighting for the gear and finally sunk under the weight of a fully loaded box of wheat. The rear axle rested on the mud. He found his gear, hit the gas and dug the entire rig even deeper. I was so glad it was Mark and not me. A fully loaded two-ton wheat truck with the rear axle sitting on sloppy mud is plenty stuck.

Mark climbed out. He was angry about getting stuck, but even angrier about the grief he was going to take for this now and later—certainly until the summer was over. Any mistake became a permanent part of your "record" with the crew and could be raised for a new round of ridicule at any moment. The men and boys on a wheat crew were as merciless as the insecure fifth graders on a playground.

We continued hauling, gunning around the buried truck and praying not to suffer the same fate. Eventually, the farmer arrived with a four-wheel drive tractor so powerful that it would pull a house off its foundation. Between the weight of the loaded truck, the depth of the mud and the marginal traction that he could gain with the tractor, the truck would not budge.

When he gave up and drove off with his mud-spattered tractor, we turned to the next option with resignation. Carefully Gary backed another truck alongside the anchored rig—box next to box—maybe one foot apart. The footing was better where the empty truck sat but not good enough to alleviate the anxiety that the same thing might happen again.

Three of us climbed in the fully loaded truck and began shoveling. An entire load of wheat, or most of it, now had to be shoveled by hand to the empty truck. Almost any boy or man can scoop grain for about two minutes. Thereafter the weight and slipperiness of the grain make for real work. Freshly harvested wheat is very heavy—a scoop-shovel full is a fight. The shovel slides so easily into the pile, but the wheat also slides so easily out of a slightly dipped shovel.

The first layer or two of wheat in this mired truck was easier because we were throwing from higher to lower—standing knee deep in a filled truck box and throwing basically down into an empty truck box. As we progressed we dropped lower and lower in the box of the mired truck and had to throw the grain up and over the box to hit the neighboring truck. For much of the afternoon we took turns shoveling and driving—some conspicuously doing more driving than shoveling.

It was heavy work, the kind of work that makes your arms and legs flood with lactic acid until they burn. It was the kind of work that made a long, boring wait in a hot, dusty, noisy truck sound wonderful. My hands and forearms ached. As the afternoon wore on, I was taking smaller and smaller scoops with the shovel just to keep going.

As we worked and the sun got high and hot, sweat drenched us and grain dust stuck to the sweat and sweat salt stung our eyes. I always loved the wonderful, musty smell of wheat, but today I tired of that smell. Our shirts and ball caps grew salt rings in ever widening circles. The sun bore down on the back of our necks—already deep brown from the summer in the sun.

As the tedious work wore on, the less than good-natured jabbing toward Mark turned to open disgust and would have soon been anger had Don not arrived. Don got in the truck and threw a few scoops into the new load. Very soon he was breathing heavily with his chest heaving. Soon after that he was gone but had stayed long enough to say that he had helped. The rest resumed our fight. We were mostly silent now. Heads down. Scoops down. Scoops up. Wheat tossed. Again and again and again. As we tired we all took smaller bites with the scoop. The progress slowed. The morale was horrible. We took longer breaks. Some guys just kept driving and never came back to take a turn at shoveling.

With nearly half the truck shoveled across, we decided to see if she would come out. We hooked a truck to the front with a heavy chain. Mark got in the truck he had stuck, and Gary got in the puller.

Gary yelled back, "Ready?'

"Hit it hard!'"

Both engines raced. Both clutches popped out. The chain took a horrendous load with a frightening snap. Nothing moved. The buried rig spun both sets of dualies in the mud of its pit and the puller truck spun both sets of dualies on the mud of the road and began to skid sideward.

Gary stopped and backed up a foot or two. "Let's hit it again," he yelled.

Same result.

Most of the guys stood close to watch the futility. For the sake of safety I got back nearly behind another truck. For as long as I can remember, I have had a morbid fear of a tow strap or chain breaking. The force exerted on the chain between one truck anchored up to the axles and the other truck full of wheat and with the accelerator floored was terrific. A weak link or a hook coming undone would cause chain to fly with the speed of a bullet and with force greater than shrapnel and with the weight of a shot put. If I wasn't in one of the trucks, I was going to be a long way off. Fortunately, no chain broke, and unfortunately, no truck moved.

On the third attempt the puller truck began to slide sideways like a water skier tethered to a boat. When Gary got too close to the fence he quit and backed up. "It ain't gonna work," he said, and no one argued. Gary unhooked and drove off for the elevator.

As we resumed our task, I silently began to cuss Mark too. I was not a kid who would say anything aloud because I didn't want to look like a whiner (though I was) or hurt the kid's feelings (though I felt like it) or risk a fist fight (which scared the tar out of me). But silently I was venting anger and frustration in floods of words, sarcastic questions, and ridicule.

In the late afternoon, with almost the entire box of wheat shifted over to the other truck, the farmer returned and pulled Dan out. The real wheels left a hole that a calf could drown in. We were all too tired to be happy.

The next day I experienced the third miserable event as we were cutting around Ness City.

In my lifetime I had been to one funeral. I could not recall seeing a severe auto accident. I had never seen a dead body. I had never witnessed a serious injury to anyone. I could count on one hand the fist fights and shoving matches that I had seen. I could count on two fingers the number of fights I had been in. I had never personally been in an auto accident. It would be hard to be more sheltered from tragedies than I was till sixteen.

Our trucks had two-way radios that worked sporadically. The whole crew used them to tell Don how long till we would be back to the field or that we had some mechanical trouble. Don used them to see where we were, to tell us to hurry or to tell us that we had moved the combines to a new field. We used them when we got separated on the highway with our combines and trailer houses. Mostly, we used them to give each other grief.

I was coming back from the elevator in Ness City and crested a rise not far from where the mirror smashing incident happened. In the middle of the road ahead of me was a big, symmetrical pile of wheat—looking like it had been intentionally piled there by an auger. Directly on top and in the middle of the mound of wheat, like a cherry carefully placed on top of a sundae, was the body of a man. In the ditch to the right of this wheat sundae was a brand new purple cab-over truck. She was on her side, belly toward the road, two wheels in the air and still spinning slowly, steam coming from the engine.

I stopped twenty yards short of the mound. For an experienced EMT this would be a run-of-the-mill call. It would be a mild incident. But for a sheltered sixteen-year-old it was not. I was frightened, stayed in my truck, and called Don on the radio—which fortunately worked at this moment. He had access to a farm phone and said he would call an ambulance. This emergency for some badly hurt man seemed to me like a nuisance to Don. His stance was simply that he would take care of it, and I should hustle back to the field.

It didn't seem right to leave the driver lying there, and I couldn't hustle back to the field without driving through a mound of wheat that had a man lying on top of it. So I stayed. After calling Don I forced myself to get out of my truck and walk up close enough to see that the man was breathing. As I got close, I could hear him moaning, but he was lying quite still. His eyes were closed, and I was not certain that he even knew I was there. The man was about thirty with very shaggy hair and a beard so thin that he should not have grown it. I was afraid he would come to and look at me and ask me to carry him or something.

I walked back and stood by my truck to wait for the ambulance. In about half an hour—which is approximately a year in emotional time—an ambulance came and two men rushed up in the mound of wheat to help. I eased around the scene with one set of tires in the ditch and one set of tires plowing through foot-deep wheat. The man looked horribly battered, and I assumed that he would not live.

The next day, I heard on the local radio station that the man was in stable condition. It surprised me. I felt guilty then, and feel amazed now, that I did not at least go up to him and try to comfort him in some way. I had no medical training—not even first aid— and I could have done nothing for him physically. However, except for my own fear, I might have been able to alleviate some of his anxiety.

Our work went on without further thought of him. Don forgot about him in five minutes. Wheat had to be cut. But I can still see him lying very still on his spilled-wheat mound. I can still see the underbelly of the capsized Ford with exposed muffler and transmission and slowly spinning tires.

I have thought of that day often. I can still see the picture of the battered man on the beautiful mound of wheat. Mainly I have thought about it because of my morbid fear of even walking up to the suffering man. Today it saddens me that I did not help in some way. Even more it amazes me that I was not willing to climb the mound or call to him or even let him know I was there. And from the moment I saw him and through every examination of that picture in my mind I wonder how he was thrown so squarely onto the top of the miniature wheat mountain. It must have been a crazy event because the final resting place of the wheat and the man and the truck does not seem possible.

In the course of our summer, as in the course of life, we encountered so many different personalities in the farmers, elevator operators, waitresses, and mechanics. One of our farmers in Ness City was a very meticulous, no-nonsense man who took his farm, his wheat, his money and his equipment with an obsessive seriousness. From the moment we stepped out of our trucks into his presence, it became clear that the safe delivery of every grain of his wheat to his private storage bins was more important than any thirty wheaties, their wallets, their watches, and their trucks combined.

From the moment I met him, I could see in him a fierce commitment to what was his and to how things must be done in his kingdom. His relational style made me feel like a five-year-old who was just caught stealing even though I was not five, had not recently stolen anything and had never stolen anything from him. He had the meticulous intensity which I came to hate in others throughout my life. I wanted to climb back in my truck and work elsewhere.

The farmers who employed us ranged along the scale from "never show up to see how it is going" to "watching every move." This man was on the "watching every move" end of the spectrum—or maybe a little beyond that end of the spectrum. And, like most people on that end of the spectrum, he was very vocal and very stern when he did not like something or someone.

I walked on eggshells around him. I simply did things the way he wanted and kept to myself. My need for compliance and for pleasing others was in overdrive, and his need for control was happy—at least with me.

Unlike many farmers he had enough storage to keep all his own wheat until the time was opportune for selling. Unfortunately, his dump bin was very narrow. It was built in such a way that our trucks had only about six inches of clearance on either side of the bed. He would not allow us wheaties to back in and insisted on backing every truck himself. Once the truck was in place and the brake was set, he would call us back to the truck so we could dump the load and then pull out of the chute.

My first time to his private granary, he stopped me and explained how it was going to work. I said, "Yes sir," and quietly moved off to the side. I stood watching him swing my truck out into the yard and begin his slow, meticulous backing—continually checking his mirrors and spacing on both sides. The nature of the man drove the nature of his choices—as is true for all of us. I was pretty cautious, but his constant mirror check and slow adjusting seemed excessive even to me.

While the farmer continued the tedious backing process, I noticed a girl about my age across the narrow track from where I was standing. She was thin and had a kind face. Beyond an embarrassing nod we did not speak to each other. While periodically stealing glances at her I pretended to concentrate very carefully on what her dad was doing. She was immeasurably more interesting than what he was doing. It was also surprising that she was in town given the fact that the wheaties were, and her dad was so exacting about his things. I assume that exacting, protective and controlling nature extended to his daughter as well.

For the second time that summer, I found myself attracted to a quiet and seemingly very confident girl. Both had a sense of self-assurance. They did not need my approval or my interest for affirmation. I had no idea what to make of this attraction, but there was something about this girl and about the waitress weeks ago that hooked me.

I thought about the girl in the farm yard a lot while I was driving back and forth from the field to the bins. On each trip I hoped she would be there. She never was.

About my second day working on this farm, one of our combine drivers spilled about a bushel of wheat in the field by failing to shut off his auger before he swung it back against his machine. He frowned but kept driving. I stopped my truck and climbed out to see this small mound of wheat on the ground and "Mr. My Wheat is Precious to Me" watching from his pickup. Immediately he drove over to the scene of the "accident," and I stiffened up.

In the volumes of wheat that we moved, a bushel was about the same as dropping a single grain of rice off the "Thursday night Chinese Wall Shrimp Stir Fry Special"—it didn't matter and no harm was really done. It was hardly worth the effort to pick it up.

"We need to pick this up," he said to me and got down on his knees by the pile. I brought my scoop and placed it beside the miniature mound of grain. We worked together and in two minutes had scooped up as much grain as we could without also scooping dirt. I pitched it carefully in the back of my truck and went to stow my scoop.

As I walked away he said to me, "That's good. Thanks." I was a little stunned but turned back and said, "You're welcome, sir."

He had not given his affirmation and thank you with anything that could be labeled "warmth," but still it had been genuine. He was apparently not a man who was capable of warmth—maybe with his daughter but certainly not with a wheatie whose name he did not know. It was one of the first times that I experienced my gift for winning over difficult people.

The next afternoon I was about third in line to dump at his narrow bin. I stood outside my truck while he backed someone's truck. When he finished, he got out of the truck and said to me, "Do you want a beer?" His question took me by terrific surprise because he clearly knew that I was underage and because I was also working—driving a truck that carried his precious wheat. It was only 3.2% beer and would take a case to get drunk, but still I was taken off guard.

I was flattered that he had warmed up to me enough to offer me a beer, and I tried to be both funny and to accept his gift at the same time. In that attempt I said to him, "Sure, as long as you don't tell Don." I really meant it to be funny because Don basically didn't care and I basically didn't care if Don knew.

But it did not come off as funny. Due to my tension it came off as defensive and frightened. He was put off by my response and said in a rather distant tone, "No, I won't tell Don."

Both the conversation and the relationship were derailed by my response, but he brought the beer to me nonetheless and had one himself. I stood there watching my truck dump, drinking a horrible-tasting 3.2% something, and feeling even more horrible that I had not simply said, "That would be great."

It was our last day in his wheat. It was my last load in his narrow chute. I got in my truck and never saw him again. I never saw his quiet daughter again.

From my first orientation to driving a wheat truck—how to back up, how to dump the wheat, how to tarp the load, how to grease the zerks, how to unload on the go, how to attach the header trailer, how to use the two-way radio, how to get weighed in and out, how to check the oil and water, how to remove and replace the box, how to load and chain down the combine, and how to use the split axles and double clutch— the most repeated and urgent instruction that Don gave to me and to all the crew was, "Always check your muffler and pipes for straw! Check every time you come into a field. Every time. The last thing I need is a fire to burn up a couple hundred acres of wheat."

Straw on the hot pipes could start a fire quickly. Every summer plenty of wheat was burned from fires that started on truck mufflers. The routine, when followed as I almost always did, was simply to pull up where you could see the combines and wait for an auger to swing out. While I waited I would shut off the motor, set the brake and crawl under the back end of the truck to see that there was no straw clogged up next to the muffler or any tail pipes. If I found straw I pulled it out—occasionally burning my hand or forearm if I got too close to the muffler or tailpipe.

One very hot afternoon outside of Ness City we were cutting a six hundred acre field which was big by our standards. The light breeze on this hot day was like sitting in front of a very large hair dryer. We had cut maybe two hundred acres, maybe a little more, and the afternoon was dragging on. All the combines chewed standing wheat and periodically spit that wheat into our trucks. When my turn came, I eased up to loaded combines, idled alongside of them while they sent a round flow of wheat into my box and headed to town with my cargo of kernels.

The elevator was ten miles or so away but the lines at the elevator were short. My turn-around time was short. On the way back to the field, I could see a small column of white smoke rising from someplace. It looked near our field but from several miles away, but I figured it could be about anywhere in the vicinity.

As I drove back, taking my various turns, the column of smoke grew substantially bigger and I knew someone had a problem. And as I got closer it was clear that Don Dexter had a problem. Our six hundred acre field was on fire. When I got to the field I could see that the fire was moving rapidly through the stubble toward the standing wheat. Don was screaming at the combine drivers to stop cutting and use their headers like bulldozers to build a fire line between the burning stubble and the standing wheat.

I parked my truck on the road and ran toward the fire. With other drivers I began fighting the fire—some of us with gunny sacks and some with scoop shovels. The gunny sacks were pulled out from under truck seats, and they were plentiful. However, they were not effective because they were dry and tended to fan the fire more than beat it down.

Don pulled someone off a combine and began to drive it wildly in front of the flames—header down, scraping straw, dirt and rock in front of him. Soon it choked out and was no longer useful for building a line. The other drivers followed Don's example and a chopped up fire line of sorts was built. The line had gaps where those of us on foot worked. After a few minutes the farmer came screaming into the field in his pick-up with some wet gunny sacks and a couple of hired hands. He had seen the smoke from his farmyard and come over in a near panic.

On foot and fighting a hot straw fire on a hot day, I got my first taste of frontline firefighting. It was my first time to feel the horrible heat of working close to the flames, to have my sweat dry quickly in the dry sauna of the fire line, to get a big gulp of smoke and back away choking, to feel the sting of smoke in my watering eyes and to have to turn away and seek clean air for a moment. Firefighting is surely one of dozens of occupations that sounds romantic and exhilarating when you are signing up. Five minutes into the actual fighting there is nothing romantic about it and the exhilaration is found in surviving.

The combines were employed as bulldozers, and one by one, they became choked with earth and straw and had to be shut down and simply moved out of the way. Slowly we gained on the blaze, and finally, forty-five minutes into the fight, we were able to declare victory.

We walked rather than ran to stomp out remaining embers or smokes. The farm hands drifted back to their work, and we as a crew took turns slithering up into the mouth of the combines to pull out straw and dirt and rocks. Like a gopher digging a hole, we lay on our bellies, reaching in front of us, fighting little pieces of earth out of the throat of the machine and pitching them partly behind us and partly on our own heads and backs.

When we were mostly ready to cut again, we stood near the service truck—drinking water to wash the dirt and smoke out of our mouths, and taking sponge baths on our heads and faces. In that gathering of ten dirty men and boys, Don said, "The fire started on me." He had stated the fact by putting himself in a passive role. Rather than admitting his error and taking responsibility for violating his own cardinal rule about checking the muffler, he had distanced himself from the mistake. After failing to do what he had drilled into each of us, he cast himself as a victim and distanced himself from fault. Even as a sixteen-year-old I felt the hypocrisy of his statement. It probably bothered me because I saw the same thing in myself too often.

The fire, the ensuing fight and the efforts to clean combines and oil the headers took three or four hours. In the late afternoon we returned to cutting—tired, filthy and educated that a fire really could start on a straw-covered muffler.

The fire day became another indelible day of the summer of '69. It was one of my first tastes of substantial threat to someone's valuable resources with the desperate responses of highly motivated men and the authentic chaos that arose. A time lapse film of those forty-five minutes would certainly show a crazy crisscross of trucks and combines and running men and flailing gunny sacks and men and machinery going back and forth and back and forth. At one moment I would be sprinting one direction because my brain was telling me that there was a need at this part of the firefight, and the next minute I would be sprinting right back to where I had been because my brain was now telling me that the crisis point had shifted.

I was mostly in the mode of visceral reacting to crisis—as was everyone. My thinking process was going too fast to track or record and way too fast to be valuable. I was thinking and I was thinking intensely. But I was also running and reacting and changing and stopping. All this was topped off with the physical threat of the fire and the roar of engines and the hollering of men and the sudden phenomenon of everyone trying to be the commander in chief. Two guys, who are peers on the non-existent organizational chart of Don Dexter Custom Harvesting, run up to each other and each give the other the identical command at the same instant as if on an Olympic-level Synchronized Commanding Team, "Jump in that truck and move it out of the way!" Do you laugh or scream? One guy does indeed run over to move the truck and the other guy runs off to do whatever he feels is important at that moment or to shout important commands at others.

In a matter of seconds a decent wheat harvest crew becomes a horrible firefighting team. At the end of that day no standing wheat was burned. However insane the process of fighting the fire looked, we won—more a testament to panicked determination than to any level of expertise or teamwork.

7 NORTH PLATTE, NEBRASKA

They were people in a fight with life –
As we all are.

North Platte, Nebraska was a good stop for me. I finally knew what I was doing as a wheat-truck driver. In and around North Platte, I did not get in any truck wrecks, did not forget to weigh out, did not bend any pulleys and did not ruin any combine belts. It felt good to develop some level of "expertise" in what was expected of me—even if not much was expected of me by most standards. I was past the frustrating break-in period of this new endeavor. For me the "I am motivated to do well but hardly know what I am doing" periods are the worst.

By now our routines as a crew were well rehearsed and gave a sense of normalcy to the summer despite constantly changing towns, constantly changing scenery, constantly changing farmers, constantly changing farms, constantly changing fields, constantly changing elevators and constantly changing routes to elevators.

My routine was to get up, find a secluded tree, roll up my sleeping bag, fold up my cot, load up my duffle, stash all three between the end of one of the bunks and the bathroom wall, get breakfast in the Dexter's trailer, get in my own truck if it was in town or in the shop truck if my truck was at the field, ride to the field, check the oil in Old Red, check the muffler for straw, grease the drive shafts if needed, get in line to unload combines and sit in my truck and think.

I was slowly coming out of my "harvest culture shock." In some ways the summer did not feel real to me. Yet in other ways the summer and the crew and the work seemed like the only real thing left in my life. It was the first of many, many times when places and people of the past seemed surreal to me. I had only been gone from home six or seven weeks but home and the routine of that life was all foggy to me. I would be back home for a one day visit in just a week, and that visit would feel very strange.

During those three months of driving trucks and following the ripening wheat, a great deal happened in the larger world. I knew about none of it—absolutely none of it. Some of the other wheaties may have known more but we never discussed matters outside our little moving circus. I knew that on a given day we were moving the machines about half a mile north to a new field, that one of the trucks had a broken spring, that lunch was going to be late getting to the field and that Don was ticked about something.

I did not know that President Nixon was withdrawing 25,000 troops from Vietnam, that Warren Burger had become the Chief Justice, or that the Stonewall Riots had occurred outside a gay bar in Greenwich Village. I had no idea that a woman named Mary Jo Kopechne had drowned in Senator Ted Kennedy's car, that Apollo 11 had landed three men on the moon, or that Muhammad Ali had been convicted of draft evasion. It was after I returned home that I learned Charles Manson and his "family" had murdered nine people, that 400,000 plus people had showed up at a farm in Bethel, New York, for a concert called Woodstock and that Hurricane Camille had killed more than two-hundred-fifty people along the Gulf Coast.

In mid-August, when the iconic Woodstock was rocking in New York, I was in Shelby, Montana driving a two-ton faded red wheat truck and hoping the laundromat would be open when I got back to town.

So many times in life our own lives become so absorbing that the bigger world—even the very near bigger world—sadly becomes of no concern to us. As a wheatie, being out of clean clothes was occupying my mind. Woodstock was not. Vietnam was not. The stock market was not. The troubles of a famous politician was not.

In North Platte, as in every town where we landed, I did laundry in the closest laundromat. I had not been in a laundromat much and had never done laundry. Since I was a baby, all the homes I lived in had a magic laundry system where I put my clothes in a laundry hamper, or just left them on the floor, and then a couple of days later they were clean, folded and back in my drawers. I knew my mom did this, but it never crossed my mind to either thank her or help her.

Each new laundry establishment in each consecutive town looked eerily the same. Rows and rows of tired washing machines on plywood risers divided the room down the middle. Generally tired dryers and occasionally a super load washing machine or two lined the walls. If there was a clerk, his plywood office was in the back. Scattered through the room were molded hard plastic chairs in various faded colors. On the chairs there were markedly out of date and well-used magazines. Occasionally a cheap photo of a sunset in a cheap frame was screwed to the wall. Tired machines bolted on the wall sold soap and laundry softener. To prevent theft, huge metal straps secured change machines already bolted on the wall. They would give patrons quarters for a dollar bill or a five dollar bill—most of the time. Usually there was a sign on the wall, painted years ago, with the prices, but most notably with the rules and instructions:

#1 No unattended machines.
#2 No saving of machines.
#3 No smoking.
#4 No loitering if you are not doing laundry.
#5 No panhandling.
#6 No unattended children.
#7 No doing something else.

and so on down to #10 or #16 or in the very obsessive shops #21. All the rules began with "No."

Somewhere in the back of the establishment were the restrooms. I classified these restrooms as "gas station restrooms" meaning that they were generally dirty. The hot water spigot had been unhooked; the mirror was cracked; the walls were covered with graffiti including limericks, filthy jokes, phone numbers and cartoons; the paint was horrible; any stalls and fixtures were hanging loose; the sinks were grungy; the toilets rocked; an ancient machine offered a variety of pleasure enhancing products for 25 cents; the paper towel dispenser was ancient and empty; the room had not had a serious cleaning since Eisenhower was president; and—at least in the men's restrooms—the smell of urine was somewhere between faint and "hold your breath till you get out if possible." Most of the doors had evidence of having been pried open. They either had no locks or a huge, metal, sliding latch that had been installed "after market." If you needed to relieve yourself in a bad way, you would probably go in. I generally stayed far away. None of these restrooms were as nice as my morning tree.

I had plenty of laundry to do owing to the dirty work and the sweat and the everyday cutting and therefore the everyday use of my work clothing. I had no "dress up clothing" with me and needed none.

Having never been trained in doing laundry, I simply found the biggest washer available and put everything in together—whites, jeans and pillow case—put in a little box of Tide or whatever detergent that particular laundromat was selling, put in my quarters and pushed the button. I usually remembered to select hot water wash and warm water rinse, and other times I got what the previous customer had selected. I had no idea what I was doing, but it was not rocket science when it came to washing a wheatie's clothes. Clean was better than dirty, and clean and a little gray was better than dirty and mostly white.

Once, I even washed my sleeping bag. It smelled wonderful the first night after that.

While waiting for my wash, I would sit in the torturous molded plastic chairs, thumb through year-old magazines or real estate magazines or novels that someone had forgotten and watch the wash go around in the round glass front of my machine. I was mesmerized by the constant motion and the ever-changing scene as my clothes washed against each other and came up in a new pattern each time they rotated and the soap swirled in psychedelic swirls and the next time around the pillowcase was above the blue t-shirt and the jeans must have fallen to the back. The machine was a laundro-kaleidoscope of entertainment for a work numbed mind.

You could easily tell the laundromat "regulars" from the tourists who had decided that they simply could not get the rest of the way home without washing. The regulars were obvious not only by their appearance but also by their general comfort level with the place and their expertise in the operation of the machines. The tourists were both inept at operating the machines and uneasy in the setting—they had a tense demeanor of "keep my back to the wall, keep my hand on my wallet and keep my eyes on my clothes."

Many, if not most, of the people in the laundromats were hard-living people with few resources. The struggle of life was evident in every feature of their appearance. They looked older than they were and often wore fatigue in their faces. Many had one to five ragged kids in tow. Their clothes were often old and worn.

The people who frequented the laundromats, while total strangers to me and to each other, were generally helpful and kind to the each other and to me. They would give you a quarter if you were one short for the dryer. They would give you soap if you had none. They would gladly move your laundry from the washer to a dryer if you wanted to walk down the street to shop or eat. They would walk over and show you the quirks of a given machine if it was not working for you. They would tell you if your washing machine had finished. They would warn you if the change machine wasn't working. They would offer you a cigarette. When I began to feel more comfortable I began to look like a regular. Once I began to look like a regular, I began to feel like family.

They were people in a fight with life—as we all are. Their particular fight was caused partly by self-destructive choices and partly by the reality of being born into a generally unfriendly universe. They recognized that I was in a fight with life—partly because of my self-destructive choices and partly because I was born into a generally unfriendly universe. They were usually street-savvy people and they looked at me quite accurately as a fresh-faced, naïve, wandering-through-life teenager, and they knew I was in a fight of my own.

And so, as people who did not know each other from a manhole cover but who needed these public washing machines, we had a camaraderie and a willingness to help each other, in whatever small way, with the fight. I almost always came out of the local washateria with a big black garbage sack full of clean clothes and a sense of having been helped and accepted.

While I felt accepted in the laundromat, I decidedly did not on the main drag where the teenagers and even younger kids of a given town drove back and forth looking for relationships and status. The people who frequented the laundromat were sufficiently marred by life that they had more compassion for others. In contrast, the people out dragging main were not yet sufficiently scarred by life to address their own arrogance and insecurities. Therefore, they were not ready to give any slack to others whom they deemed below them for any reason—race, age, income, handicap, occupation, or "not being from around here."

One night, having finished our cutting and hauling very early—owing to finishing a field and it being too late to move to the next—we got home in time to do something, though I had no particular plan. I showered and found a clean shirt. After supper and after dark around ten, Mark, Dan and I borrowed the shop truck and went to "drag main" in North Platte. It did not take long to find "the drag" which was plenty busy on a summer evening in this plains town.

We joined a ritual for that one June night that has been practiced for uncountable nights in uncountable towns by uncountable kids with uncountable vehicles—dragging main. Back and forth on the traditional "main" route in each given town, mostly but not exclusively, young people were on the lookout for something to do or someone to meet. They were in hot cars, average cars, borrowed cars, old cars, pickups, dad's cars and even wheatie shop trucks. The agenda was, at the core, just be where things were happening. Further agendas included impressing others with cars or appearances, finding someone to drag race, getting out of the house and away from parents and siblings, meeting someone or finding someone you know or really want to know. Dragging main was about relationship—some healthy and some not. Dragging main was about status—some having it; some not having it, but wanting it; some thinking they had it but did not.

Dragging main in every town had basically the same elements. The periodic squeal of tires exhibited someone who could not resist the urge to "get in the carburetor" of their hot car or their dad's station wagon. Occasionally, there would be a fist fight over a girl or a past event or some miss-chosen` words or an unpaid loan. There were shouts and hand gestures. Loud music came from various cars and pickups. Rarely there was a "cat fight" as two girls allowed their rage at each other to overwhelm their desire to maintain some image or another. Generally, there was a patrol car or two in the mix. They cruised slowly which caused the other traffic to cruise slowly. Though generally the idea in dragging main was to cruise slowly in order to see and be seen. At times one of the officers would make a "stop" either as a "let this be a warning to you" gesture or because they suspected drugs, underage drinking or some young, tough kid driving without a license. At times a stop was just to harass the cop's nephew or embarrass a friend or ask a question of another friend. Dragging main in North Platte and the towns where we cut wheat generally involved a few wheaties whom no one knew and a regular cast whom everyone knew.

The fronts of closed stores, vacant lots or the lot of a drive-in were the designated "parking lots." These were full of cars parked in a jangled mess like a box of toys that that had been dropped. Teens hung in groups talking, joking and jockeying for proximity next to the cute girls. 3.2% beer was sipped discreetly. Conversations ran heavily to sports and relationships and girls and guys and cars and farming and summer jobs and plans for the fall. Smoking happened cautiously among the underage and openly among the "of age." Periodically a teen boy would walk away from a group, spit a stream of tobacco juice into a garbage can or behind a car and return to the group. Occasionally, a girl would do the same.

Back and forth we went in a seemingly meaningless ritual of youth—part habit, part mating, part bragging, part tagging along, part getting out of the house, part arranging of pecking order, part figuring out personal identity, and part just being in the middle of summer life. Dragging main was ten-fold better than sitting on the porch with the folks.

On our first pass down the street, someone from a lot yelled, "Nice car!" when we passed. Mark responded with the appropriate hand gesture. Laughter ensued from both the lot and our truck.

A little later Mark slowed the shop truck and then stopped to talk to three girls parked in a new pickup truck—clearly borrowed from Daddy. Mark must have figured, three of them and three of us and no other guys around—this is worth a stop.

"How are ya?" Mark said really quite naturally.

"We're good," one of them replied and all three smiled with the embarrassed smile of a main drag encounter with three total strangers—and wheaties no less. A self-respecting local guy with any other option at all would not show up in a shop truck.

"Whatcha doin' tonight?" was Mark's next question.

The same girl, apparently the spokeswoman owing to her greater boldness, answered, "Just drivin' around."

"You wanna do something, go get a coke maybe?" offered Mark.

"I don't know," she said and turned to talk to her friends. Certainly the invitation was a little more than they had bargained for coming so quickly from three total strangers in an out of state truck.

Mark turned to us and asked, "What do you guys think?"

Before Dan could say anything, I said, "I think they're ugly. Let's get outta here."

Mark and Dan both looked at me like I was insane, but neither said anything.

Mark turned back to the three girls who were still conversing which was not a good sign. Feeling the embarrassment of being turned down not with words but with delay, Mark finally said, "Hey, maybe another time."

"Sure, maybe," was the reply.

We pulled away as the girls giggled. All six of us knew we would never see each other again unless maybe we passed on the drag sometime later that night. It was one of eighty billion attempted male-female connections that never happened. But three on three between total strangers is poor odds for a connection.

We drove around for another hour. Nothing happened, and we talked to no one else. Mark turned off the drag toward our trailer court, and we called it a night. In the two hours on the drag we had talked to one girl, burned some gas, been ridiculed once for driving the shop truck, seen the local scene and been there.

I lay on my cot that night, less sleepy than normal and looking at the stars visible between the trees and the top of the trailer, and thought about my instant reply. "I think they're ugly. Let's get outta here." I was insanely anxious at the moment I said it—in fact that is why I said it.

Those three girls were attractive, not ugly at all, and I knew it. Rather than being ugly, the girls were frightening to me. The more honest response to Mark would have been, "They scare me. Let's get outta here!" My heart was racing at the thought of getting out of the truck and sitting down with them, even in the company of Mark and Dan, in a booth and trying to look handsome and cool and relaxed at the same time. The setting felt like seeing the snake ssss'ing across my path next to my cot back in Alva. My basic experience in those settings was tension and raw embarrassment. I could think of nothing to say. When I said something, it sounded forced and strange. When I tried to be funny, it was stupid. I suffered such personal insecurity that I projected that insecurity into the middle of these boy-girl settings. I struggled with my anxieties—anxieties related to girls and snakes and injured men and flying mirror fragments and darkness and not keeping track of my hours and forgetting to weigh my truck and bending pulleys and my dad's approval and my coach's anger and the list goes on.

It is strange that a boy who would be hooked so powerfully by the words "travel required" would also be so covered over with anxieties and fears and situational timidity—and with obsessive focus.

I fell asleep thinking about these things and woke in the morning with my head down in my sleeping bag and dew covering it. I went quickly to my trees of choice, got dressed for the day and gathered up my gear. I was still thinking about the encounter with three pretty girls in a pickup truck.

As I stashed my bag, cot and duffle in their usual place in the trailer, I was struck with the filthiness of the place. I had been in there two hundred times, but for some reason it seemed like walking in for the first time and being hit with the sensations that greet "new eyes" as they look on an unfamiliar scene.

The trailer was at least twenty years-old, and they had not been easy years. Outside the skin was simple, flat aluminum. The trailer, even new, was a simple and bottom-of-the-line, no-frills model.

By now this trailer, which had never been clean or nice, was showing the wear of almost two months with eight or nine wheaties living inside. Socks, long ago orphaned in a corner or under a bed, were overlooked and became as much a fixture as the cheap lights screwed on the walls. Beds were never made—except for Mark's and Cliff's. Ancient suitcases peeked out from under bunks and ball caps hung on the corners of bunks and on light fixtures. Boots gathered in a jumbled pile at the front door. Cigarette butts were scattered across the floor from a spilled ash tray. Beer cans were ubiquitous. Occasionally "reading material" would appear and then disappear under someone's mattress.

Beyond the visual repulsiveness of the place was the smell. A person who ever experienced a football locker eight weeks into the season and the smell of the uniforms, jockstraps, and socks had never been washed would know the smell of our crew trailer. In addition the shower room smelled musty and the toilet room smelled of urine. I did not know how the guys slept in this trailer. Maybe it was the familiarity like that of a family who no longer notices the horrible mustiness of their own basement. I was again glad to be the "odd man out" and in this case outside on a cot that I could locate at the most agreeable place.

Mark was coming out as I came in. "Morning," I said, and he did not respond to my greeting. He was not mad at me; he was just growing more impatient and less personable as the summer wore on. This was his fourth year as a wheatie in the employment of Don Dexter, and it was also decidedly his last. Perhaps he was beginning to feel the end of an experience that had started well, but was now very tedious. In about six more weeks, he would put the experience behind him for good. By this time next year, he would be a graduate engineer who had done his time in the wheat fields and the heat and the slums of the wheatie trailer.

By this time next year, Mark planned to be searching for a good engineering job, drawing a good salary and married to his girlfriend. Most of all, he would be done with truck drivers who lied to him, combine drivers who hated him, chaff in the tops of his socks, wearing a hat every waking minute to keep his dark hair from being bleached, Marie whining at him and Don not carrying his share of the load.

As for me I was still very happy with my decision to let my hair get bleached out. It was getting longer and longer and fully white. I was a very young Buffalo Bill—without any facial hair. I did not have any facial hair because to my deep dismay I could not grow any. I was shaving to keep the twelve or so blond hairs in front of my ears from looking goofy. That was all I had, and it bothered me. But I did have my white hair and would often sit outside the cab in the sun both to keep my hair white and to escape the oven-like feel of the cab.

The cab of my truck could be so hot when there were no clouds at all. Once in awhile when smaller clouds were drifting by there was a short relief of being in the shade for a minute or a few minutes. I remember my Mom talking about growing up on the prairie homestead in South Dakota and loving the shade under small clouds that would drift by on hot summer days. Mom and her sisters would run in the short grass of the prairie to stay under the cloud as long as they could before it would outdistance them and leave them in the summer sun again.

Sitting in the cab one day in North Platte, waiting for the signal of an outstretched auger, it struck me how much harvesting caused me to focus on the weather. For us in custom harvesting so much depended on the "right" weather. So much was riding on avoiding hail and heavy wind and violent thunderstorms. So much of the comfort or discomfort of the day depended on the temperatures and the speed of the wind. On backpacking trips with my Dad and my brother, I had a similar focus on weather. In both cases I found myself repeatedly checking the sky for signs of clouds or rising wind or forming thunder cells. The wrong formations beginning in the sky or drifting in from the distance caused concern in Don, the farmers, and even us wheaties.

The average tourist traveling through North Platte on the way from Florida to Yellowstone Park did not give much thought to the weather. If it rained they would turn on the wipers. If the wind blew the driving would be a little unpleasant. It was not going to snow, and they had both windshield wipers and roll-up windows in the event of rain.

The very same event—a thunderstorm for example—has starkly different meanings for a tourist than for a custom harvester. So much of life is driven by our individual goals and dreams and perspectives and the constraints of our various livelihoods. A thunderstorm does not keep a tourist from getting to Yellowstone, but it could easily keep a field from being cut today or even tomorrow.

I was snapped out of this reflection by the sight of Cliff's auger swinging out. I turned the key, pulled into gear and eased over behind his combine. When I was still behind his lumbering machine but gaining on him, I opened my door and stood up. Soon I was beside him, and the auger was squarely over the box of Old Red. I nodded at Cliff, and he turned on the flowing wheat.

As I looked back—attending to the flow and placement of the wheat—I watched Dan in the combine behind us. He was maybe thirty yards back, but I could clearly see him singing and swaying his head and automatically driving his combine.

Dan had calmed considerably since the start of summer. He was far less agitated and had abandoned his incessant use of shock speech and had become rather quiet—at least for Dan. He surprised me in how easily and consistently he slid into his apparently boring job as a combine driver. Something in the pace or the noise or the loneliness of it seemed to soothe his soul and he climbed up every day with no apparent reluctance—in fact almost with real ease and contentment. His great intelligence and terrific aptitude for imagination gave him all he needed to spend the hours upon hours in what could mostly be a mindless job.

Barring a fire or a truck running into the side of his header, Dan had learned to zone out on the machine—to drive with skill and with the natural ease of a veteran bike rider who shifts gears because he needs to even though his brain does not even register that he has done it. Dan adjusted his header and his speed because he needed to and without breaking stride in "I Heard it through the Grapevine" or Pinball Wizard" or "Time of the Season." In his head, and with his voice though thoroughly drowned out by the harvesting machine, "It's the time of the season for loving. / What's your name? / Who's your daddy? / Is he rich like me? / Has he taken any time / to show you what you need to live? / Tell it to me slowly. / Tell you what I really want to know. / It's the time of the season for loving." The Zombies, Marvin Gaye, The Rolling Stones and Steppenwolf entertained Dan much of the summer. When these groups were unavailable, Dan always had the theater of his own mind.

While Dan had settled in nicely, Marie was growing more and more agitated with the dragging summer. She was plenty vocal about her hatred of cooking and plenty open about her suspicions about Don. She was also greatly unappreciated by Don and most of the crew and she knew it. I and an occasional other wheatie would thank her or even compliment her on a meal and it would bring obvious light to her face. She seemed to be starved for appreciation, adult conversation, and a happy relationship with her husband. These things were a lot to be without, and she wore this lack poorly.

At the beginning of the summer, jaded by Mark's description of her, put off by her anger, and unfamiliar with her lot in the custom harvesting life, I had been critical of Marie and harbored hidden disdain for her. At least, I think it was hidden. As the summer progressed her pain and fears became clearer to me and I began to develop compassion for her. I now saw her as a person who was thoroughly unappreciated and who deserved better than the way she was treated, especially by her husband.

She must have had friends back in Alva. I had paid no attention to that question. For all I could tell she had none on the harvest route. How many times she had been on this route I did not know. Whatever the number she occupied herself, by choice or by necessity, completely with her responsibilities and not with friendships.

Judging from the prosperity of their farm outside Alva, it looked as if Marie was well taken care of financially. Emotionally and relationally, she was not.

One morning in North Platte, we got up to the news that Marie was not cooking today and that we should walk together down to a café near us. "Marie's not cooking today," was Don's simple message. "Is she sick?" I asked him and immediately wished I had not. "She is just taking a day off!" he replied hotly. There was plenty of speculation about this development, but the truth was never known to us.

Thinking about all that Marie had—family, farm, income, and possessions—I at first felt her to be either greedy or ungrateful or both. As the summer wore on it became clear to me that she would have traded all but her children for the love of her husband.

The café was busy but we found two tables and shoved them together with no small amount of disruption to the people around us. Breakfast took a long time—we waited for a waitress and then waited for our food. We had plenty of time to sit and watch people and listen to the farm report. Local stations in North Platte, Ness City and every farm community that had a local radio were razor focused on what mattered to farm people. The announcers were generally older men, quite polished in their work, and often fountains of western sayings and one-liners.

What mattered to farm people was the weather, wheat yield projections, the price of pork bellies, and the sale price of yearlings and heifers, the status of a farm subsidy bill and the scores of any local sports events—high school in the fall, winter, and spring and American Legion Baseball in the summer. To a teen who did not care about the local American Legion team and who did not know what a pork belly was, the stations were not enjoyable listening.

This café, like most, had the usual suspects for a summer morning in ag country—"ag country" being the universal abbreviation for agricultural country. There were waitresses and cooks in their recognizable uniforms, farmers and ranchers in their recognizable uniforms, wheaties in their recognizable uniforms, and, rarely, tourists in their recognizable uniforms. Without having ever laid eyes on each other before, we all knew who everybody else was. A convict walking in with a black and white striped suit would have been recognized by his uniform but no more than the waitress in her white blouse, white skirt, and short blue apron.

The forty waitresses we met that summer mostly fell in two

categories. The first category was the teenage girls doing summer work. They were generally outgoing, helpful, and hardworking. When the place was busy they could get flustered quickly. They usually knew the menu though occasionally they would look over your shoulder after you ordered and say, "I think you get hash browns with that."

The other category was the "journey-woman waitress." These women were between thirty and seventy-five and most had been waiting tables for a long time. They called the locals by their first names and almost everyone else "hon." They worked their tables with an ease that grew from years of experience—an unhurried but always moving rhythm of a person who not only knew what they were doing, but who also had moved to a level of efficiency and expertise where they could do the next thing, do things in the right order and do two things at once. They operated without apparent stress in a setting that would cause panic in a brand new waitress, or in me.

These journeywoman knew the menu so well they could have sat down at a table and reproduced it on napkins. When you ordered say a "Number Four" they would immediately say, "How do you want your eggs?" and then, "Sausage or bacon?" and then, "Link or patty?" and then, "Hash browns, grits, or pancakes?" and then, "White, wheat, or sourdough toast?" and then, "Anything to drink besides coffee?" The simple matter of ordering the "Number Four" left you exhausted from decision making.

These journeywoman waitresses filled an important niche in most towns. The part of their job that seemed central—waiting tables—was unconsciously easy to them, the same as driving a combine was to Dan. The rest of their job included listening to troubles, jabbing and counter-jabbing with customers, giving a word of encouragement to a struggling customer, passing on new jokes, and acting as a clearinghouse for other information—true or rumored—that anyone might need to know or want to know or want to pass on. They were part of the glue of the community and most of them loved their roles. They were the flirts, the surrogate grandmothers or the mothers insisting that you eat your fruit, the news reporter telling you about the accident last night or all three in the course of a single meal.

I came to see that even the "grumpy" women were well-loved and well-accepted in their own café and town. Most of the regulars happily took on the challenge of cheering up or riling up the grumpier waitresses. The regulars didn't care if they made the old biddy really mad because they didn't have to go home to her that night.

A farmer would start the exchange by shouting, "How about a refill

Dorothy?" And Dorothy would say, "Hell, I'm busy Bud. Get up and get it yourself!" Her voice would be full of real or feigned anger. Then Bud would say, "Why the hell do they have waitresses in this place if we have to fill our own coffee?" This was followed by a generous round of laughter from Bud and his fellow farmers. "We have waitresses here mostly to babysit farmers and throw out the occasional smartass!" Now Bud was one down and the object of the laughter. "You are probably the only one in here who could throw a man like me out of here, Dorothy!" was Bud's return volley. "My grandmother could have thrown you out when she was in her wheelchair!" was Dorothy's comeback as she passed with someone's order. Everyone was entertained for no extra charge.

We wrapped up in North Platte. I don't know why I enjoyed the town, other than the cutting went well and the town was a little bigger and I got to drag Main for my one time that summer. And, while acting very angry, a real nice woman in her seventies called me "hon" about fourteen times in one morning.

When we had the combines loaded and the header trailers on, we took our entire caravan to gas up. It was a chore since Don liked to put all the gas on one or two pumps and pay with one credit card. That meant stretching our connected menagerie out in a long line and choking the station for some time and even affecting the traffic on the street. To fill every tank we had to parade four trucks, two pickups, a shop truck and Marie's station wagon past one or two pumps. That would have been bad enough, but we added to that four header trailers and two house trailers. Whoever owned the place made a little money, but the clerks and other customers were in for a half-hour headache.

I never saw one of Don's bills for fueling the entire fleet. To me the numbers of custom harvesting were staggering. The amount of money that Don spent was surely a great deal less than the amount of money he made—and he spent a lot. My own finances were at a level, and had always been at a level, that made it impossible for me to even imagine what it was like to have a lot of money, earn a lot of money, and to spend a lot of money. Watching Don's bill climb up at the gas pumps was fascinating to me as a $1.50-an-hour wheatie.

I was happy to be moving up to South Dakota. We would be close enough to Nemo to visit my family. The visit would turn out to be, or at least to feel, pretty strange.

North Platte grew smaller and then disappeared in the make-do mirror that was still taped on Old Red.

As I watched the horizon for the first sighting of the Black Hills I had the sudden feeling that I was a bit player in all the settings where I found myself—in the laundromat, on the main drag, in the café, and even on the harvest crew. I seemed so often to be the one watching the play from the middle of the play. People who mattered were acting and being acted upon all around me. But I was just there, watching. Even when I had a part or took initiative to say my lines the other actors and actresses just tolerated me. They hardly noticed me. They did not show noticeable disdain for me but dismissed me with a casualness that made neither me nor them think anything of it. Being dismissed, or more accurately not mattering, was a way of life for me as a child and now I must have brought this mindset along to my summer journey.

The summer was closing in on half over, and I had finally hit my stride. I was not afraid of screwing up something. I was not anxious about the members of the crew. I was not as homesick as I had been. I was not yet feeling the "short-timer syndrome" that so often plagued me in life. I was in what was for me a rare "sweet spot." How much better my summer—and my life—would have been if I had learned to simply create the "sweet spot" when I was in any spot.

8 NEMO, SOUTH DAKOTA

It was one of the few times in my life
When timidity served me well.

A huge field of ripe wheat rippling in the sunshine and the breeze is nothing short of beautiful. The golden color and the wind-driven waves moving through the sea of standing grain mesmerize. Countless writers and poets have compared ripe wheat to the ocean for obvious reasons. Farmers certainly appreciate the beauty of a ripe, rippling field of wheat. But when a farmer and a poet look at a beautiful field the farmer is far more anxious than the poet. The poet can keep the scene in his mind. The farmer needs the kernels in his elevator.

Standing in the field, ripe and full and beautiful, wheat is as vulnerable as a baseball cap in a hurricane. The main predators of wheat are wind, hail, and rain. Fire is a predator as well, but far less common than damaging weather. On more than one occasion our crew left a partly cut beautifully standing field one night and returned to a matted-down, bent over, water-laden, uneven, sickening mess—the product of wind or rain or hail or all three. What had yesterday been a yellow sea of money was today a near total loss. Some grain could be salvaged but the loss was always substantial and for the farmer it was disheartening. The decision to not cut later in the night is a slight gamble. Usually the gamble pays off. But sometimes the huge circular blotches of matted-down wheat scattered around the field signal that your number did not hit. So much is riding on the safe harvest of tons of little yellow kernels. A safe harvest is a big payoff. A lost harvest is a big setback—at times a "we're going to lose the farm" setback.

When a person without agricultural background wanders through the bakery section of a supermarket, they only see a sea of options in bread varieties. Farmers walking through those stores see relief. They could never breathe easy until the wheat was fully stored—in their own granaries or in the local elevator. At that point the threat of weather was gone and the waiting game for optimum prices began—one enemy down and one to go.

Wheat prices, like most farm commodities, can fluctuate—sometimes drastically depending on crop yields, weather hazards, market conditions, and yields around the country or even world market competition. Selling at the right time can mean windfall profits, and not selling at the right time can mean bankruptcy. Gambling on selling at the right price joins the long list of farming gambles—weather, fuel prices, machinery breakdowns, changes in government subsidy programs, yield and timing. As a bumper sticker on the back of a farm pickup reads, "Legalize gambling! Why should farmers have all the fun?"

In the constant motion of wheat harvesting, the summer in some ways became a blur to me. Get up. Eat. Get to the field. Get greased. Wait for the moisture content to drop. Cut. Haul. Shut down. Get to town. Shower. Sleep. Do it all again the next day and the next and the next. On most days a wheatie could not really tell you the day of the week or the date of the month. We could say that it was early July or mid-August—we knew that much.

Custom harvesting is an occupation where you just go and go and go as long as the conditions are right. When the wheat is ripe, it must be cut. The window for successful harvest, and thus for making money, is limited and defined. Taking off a day here and there was not an option. Like a commercial fishing season that is open for a few hours or a few days or a few weeks—just go and go and go. Custom harvesting is the "Poster Occupation" for the proverb, "Make hay while the sun shines."

We had one true day off in the three months that I drove truck for Don Dexter Custom Harvesting: the Fourth of July. Three or four other days during that summer we did not work much due to rain. Since rain days were unpredictable, we had little opportunity to go anywhere or do anything or plan anything. On the few rain days we had, Don insisted we do all the machinery maintenance before we wandered off to drink in the local bars, read or sleep. On those days I read a little, slept a lot, and was bored a lot.

I had no transportation and I was accustomed to having none. I could go as far as I wanted to walk or hitchhike. I could borrow a vehicle or I could stay where I was. It was on one of those days without wheels that I walked around the perimeter of Don's massive empty machine shed and looked at the forty years of accumulated farming stuff—the flotsam and jetsam of four decades of wheat farming. This was before I had eight dozen things I would have loved to do with a free day. It was before I was a reader to speak of. It was before discretionary time had become like gold to me. I was accustomed to burning time like it was a ruined cardboard box.

That first week of July we were cutting just east of the Black Hills of South Dakota and only eighty miles from my home in Nemo, South Dakota. Nemo is a little town twenty-two miles northwest of Rapid City. It consisted of a dude ranch, a school for grades kindergarten through eight, a few scattered homes, and a little store/restaurant/US Post Office. "When the mail was in," Nemo had eighty people. On an average afternoon you could scarcely field a football team with the residents.

Our family actually lived three miles outside of Nemo at the Boxelder Job Corps Center which was run by the US Forest Service. The Job Corps was designed to give inner city, underprivileged kids a place to get away from violence and drugs and learn a trade. The "kids" were actually eighteen and older. They came to the Black Hills from Chicago and New York and LA. Leaving the projects in some urban setting then landing at Boxelder Job Corps Center was a major shock to most of them.

The "corpsmen" at Boxelder could learn to weld or cook or do carpentry or drive heavy equipment or be an administrator. My dad was the director of Boxelder as one of his many assignments with the US Forest Service. Our home was on the center property at the end of a short gravel road and surrounded by Ponderosa Pine forest. It was only one hundred yards above a nice trout stream and in the middle of numerous four-wheel drive trails—many of which my brother and I traveled in my dad's Ford Bronco and mostly without my father's knowledge. It was a great place to live as a sixteen-year-old. It was rough on my Dad's Bronco.

On this one day off for the summer, I borrowed the shop truck and together with Dan and Cliff drove to my house outside of Nemo. Wanting to surprise my family I didn't tell anyone I was coming. I had very little communication with my folks up to that point having written maybe one letter and called maybe twice. My mother was a wonderful letter writer, but had no address to reach me as I hop-scotched from

Oklahoma to the north and west.

When I pulled up in front of our government-issued house in the Ponderosa Pine forest, my brother Alan happened to be looking out the picture window as we parked. When we wheaties piled out to walk up to the door, my brother said to my mom, "There are three hippies here in a pickup truck."

My mother immediately responded, even before seeing me, "It's probably David."

Between longer, whiter hair and strange, ragged friends, my brother did not recognize me. Hippie was not a particularly flattering label in his mental category. Luckily for me I was a wheatie—likely a notch down from a hippie.

The three of us sat in the living room with Mom and my four siblings, drank lemonade and talked for a bit. Even though it was the Fourth of July and my dad was off work, he was gone somewhere. There was not much to say sitting with two starkly different groups of people—my family of origin and two wheaties. It was another one of those awkward settings where the relationships and contexts of the two groups were so diverse that the conversation was limited. I was the only common denominator between two very distant groups. Things I might have liked to tell my family could not be spoken in front of the wheaties. Things I might have told the wheaties about my family could not be said either. It was like being at a party with your high school friends and your parents—everyone may have been amiable, but no one was having fun. Dan was the common denominator from the last time this had happened to me. My siblings stayed in the room but did not talk. My sisters were still processing their brother looking like he did and driving away in a borrowed truck with two strangers. They wore a look of confusion as they studied me—long hair bleached white by the sun and strange friends and faded jeans and a t-shirt that was no longer even close to white. They had nothing to say or ask. They just wanted to watch and listen. My mother, more gracious and more socially skilled than all of us together, carried the conversation by asking questions and making observations.

I got up to dismiss myself and my friends when my Mom insisted on packing a lunch for us. She was ever kind and generous, and like many mothers of her generation, said, "I love you." with food. We hung around awkwardly while she put together her standard terrific lunch, said goodbye and went back to the shop truck.

Dan, Cliff and I planned to eat our lunch at Pactola Reservoir only twenty-five miles from our house. Pactola Reservoir is the largest dam and lake in the Black Hills. It is named after the abandoned mining town of Pactola that was buried in water when the dam was completed in 1956. Pactola was founded in 1875 and thrived as a gold mining town. It boasted the first hotel ever built in the Black Hills, a railroad, and a beautiful meadow next to Rapid Creek. Rapid Creek runs in and out of the lake which serves for both water supply and flood control. It is full of water for most of the year and full of childhood memories for me.

As a grade schooler I loved Pactola Lake. It was one of the few places when I felt carefree, and even as a child I seldom felt that. Being given to worry and responsibility—except when it came to school work and teeth brushing—I carried a heavy burden that no one had placed on me except me. At Pactola, I could swim and skip rocks and explore along the beach or up into the forest. Our family drove there on Sunday afternoons. My father loved the woods. He worked in the woods Monday through Friday. He hunted or fished in the woods on Saturday. He drove the family out into the woods on Sunday.

At Pactola my siblings and I could float on inner tubes out into the lake until Mom screamed out to us, "You kids come back toward shore!" We roasted hot dogs and dozed on the beach. We built forts on the beach out of sticks and rocks and then destroyed them in one mighty barrage of kicking feet and yelling. I ran and played and gulped water while swimming and ate too much watermelon. I had no idea what a mortgage was, I didn't know the word "divorce," and I had never heard of insurance premiums. At Pactola on those summer afternoons, I was a kid.

On this Fourth of July I did none of the "kid's stuff." It was a sad day off. Here is the Fourth of July and my only day off for the entire summer, and I just ate with my friends as we sat on top of a picnic table watching the families do what families do on the Fourth of July. The lake was crowded. We were observers like play-goers watching a drama or comedy on stage. No matter how good the play, we were not in it— the anticlimactic day when you expect something fun and nothing materializes. Worse yet you feel like a child who was not picked for kickball. Worse yet you feel like a spectator of life—on a very enjoyable life that you cannot be part of.

Sitting on a picnic table and watching the family festivities brought back to my memory one of the great injustices of my childhood. It involved my brother. Al had a friend whose dad was wealthy and who had a boat. This family spent many weekends on Pactola Lake with the boat. They fished and water skied and camped and had camp fires—in short they had lots of fun. Since Al was friends with one of their boys, he was often invited along on these outings. He had great fun and came home to tell me tales of boating and fishing and camp fires. Worst of all, the height of injustice, is that he learned to water ski, and I had never even had a chance to try. Al sensed his "one-upmanship" in the constant competition between two brothers who were only twenty months apart. I had not forgiven him. Now, on that afternoon years after the incident, I sat there amazed at how this could be a towering injustice to me when I was seven and a joke now I was sixteen. As I thought back on it I could not imagine why I cared. It was my first taste of the perspective of "age."

When our lunch was done we got in the shop truck and drove through the Needles and past Mount Rushmore and back to the trailer. We couldn't think of anything else to do. Like the proverbial cat that went to London only to chase mice in the castle, we went back to the trailer.

The day served to highlight my homesickness. Though I longed to be launched and adventurous, I was also periodically homesick— periodically very homesick. That strange combination was wrestling inside me. Like a tribal boy who wants to stay with his mother in her lodge and also wants to go with his dad and the warriors to the men's lodge—stuck in the transition time.

At times during the summer I would feel responsible and capable and adventurous. At other times I would nurture the homesickness in my mind and heart to the point of tears. Thinking about my family, my home and my school caused me to spin myself down into misery—and really for no reason. I was very good at this activity. The images of home, of me being lost and distant, and of sadness that I created in my mind were epic. My gift for nurturing personal sadness and wallowing in misery made it all far worse than it really was. I spent whole days needlessly and helplessly in misery while obsessing about not being home and how much I loved home and why I had left home and how many days till I went home.

As we drove east and back to the trailer from Pactola that day, I watched the Black Hills getting smaller and smaller in the shop truck's rear view mirror. That steadily decreasing view of the Hills became my metaphor for homesickness for the rest of the summer. In six short weeks I would be back at home and back at school. I wasted emotional energy thinking about home and my family and school—the very things I thought I wanted to escape.

I can still see the diminishing Black Hills in that mirror and still feel a twinge of sadness. That image somehow lodged in my soul not as a picture of longing to be back in my family of origin but as a picture of sad things—losing my mother and the first week of our empty nest and leaving my career of 29 years.

On July fifth, after my dismal day off, I had an incident with my truck that was caused by me making two mistakes together—both could have been avoided and would have been avoided by someone more responsible than me, a teen who had been driving a truck for just a few weeks. If I had made one mistake or the other, there would have been no problem. But, as with so many things in life, it was the combination of mistakes that gave me trouble.

A loaded wheat truck, especially an old one, is tough to get moving and tough to keep moving. It simply takes a lot of power to overcome the inertia of a load like that and to keep it rolling. Only in rare settings can the truck get any real speed. Good downhill sections of road were one of those rare settings for any speed above about forty-five miles per hour in my truck.

I dutifully checked the oil in Old Red on most days and more days than not added a quart. She was burning a little and leaking a little, but she was also pressing on with the energy she had. One of the things I admired in trucks and in people was persistence. Old Red had that.

Having checked the oil on one of the final days of cutting in South Dakota, I let the hood fall on her tired hinges and springs and jumped in for the day of hauling. It was a "nothing happening and nothing new" kind of day that so many of the harvest days were. Most all of them were now, causing me to consider myself a "veteran" wheatie. It was a day that mostly blended into the memory of dozens of days that were hard to separate from each other unless some unusual thing happened like getting a mirror smashed in your face, seeing a near-dead man on a pile of wheat or being "cooled down" by a policeman while I shivered in a swimming pool.

The one exception to this location is that the haul to town sent us down a very long and perfectly straight steep hill on a gravel road. Maybe a mile after the hill leveled out at the bottom, the road turned to blacktop and we turned right to head for the elevator in town.

On most of my loads I approached the long gravel hill cautiously, geared down, and used my brakes periodically to keep my speed safe. I had been taught by my dad, who taught me to drive in our old rag-top jeep when I was twelve, how to drive downhill. He taught me to shift into a lower gear and make the engine work against the hill—essentially making a brake out of the engine. He taught me that you can't ride the brakes steady because they will overheat and warp the brake parts—if not burn them up altogether. You have to get on the brakes and get on them pretty good for a short stretch and then get off them completely to let them cool. Then you can get on them again if you need to.

This morning my familiarity with the hill and a need to feel some speed motivated me to let the loaded truck run down the hill. I didn't gear down and I didn't bother with the brakes. It seemed safe enough actually. The ditches were not deep. There was nothing at the bottom to hit. It was more than a mile from the bottom of the hill to the paved road. No one was coming. So, given that is was so "safe," I let it roll.

That initial feeling of safety began to dissipate as the weight of the truck and load of wheat pushed the speed up and up to near sixty miles per hour. That speed in a heavily loaded wheat truck on a gravel road with worn out shocks and springs was too much, and I knew it. I held the wheel steady and gently got on my brakes. There was no thought at all of downshifting because the speed of the engine and the speed of the truck would never allow me to get into a lower gear. Besides, I was too scared by this time to take even one hand off the wheel. And I knew better than to brake hard.

Old Red was spitting gravel off both directions. The vibration was major. The momentum that I felt in the seat of the truck was frightening.

Almost everyone at some point in their childhood has gone too fast down a hill on a bike or a sled. And anyone who had done that can remember the terrifying feeling of just trying to hold their bike or sled—which suddenly felt very flimsy and vulnerable—steady and straight until the hill leveled out at the bottom—thus saving their own life.

This was my feeling as I rocketed down this gravel road, but multiplied by several tons. The truck was not flimsy, it was very sturdy. But I had clearly sacrificed full control of the rig. I had some control of the steering though that was compromised on gravel. I had given up control of my speed.

I was now halfway down the hill and had a good half a mile left before the road leveled out at the bottom when the hood of my truck bounced open.

I had not adequately shut the hood when I checked the oil that morning. The sixty mile an hour wind that I had created by letting Old Red run now peeled that hood up, overpowered the hinges and springs and pasted the hood flat against the windshield. Now, in addition to going more than sixty miles per hour down a gravel road with a fully loaded wheat truck in high gear, all I could see was a faded red hood two feet in front of me. That was all.

All I could think to do was keep the wheel as straight as possible and use the brakes sparingly. Like a kid on an overloaded bike, I just tried to hold her straight and steady until the hill flattened out at the bottom— thus saving my own life. The problem being of course that I was not at all sure what was "straight." I could hold her "steady" and actually be going into the ditch.

I looked out my side window to judge my distance from the ditch— that made it almost worse. The ditch was moving past me at sixty miles per hour, and judging distance using a ditch as a steering mechanism was even more unnerving.

In the mercy of God on a foolish kid, I did hold her steady and straight enough. When the hill leveled out to totally flat gravel I got on the brakes as much as I dared so as not to send the several ton monster into a slide. When the truck slowed even more I poked my head out the window to see myself fairly well in the middle of the road. I pulled into the right hand ditch and shut off the truck. My heart did not slow for a long, long time. I kept my sweating palms on the skinny steering wheel and recovered.

Climbing out of the truck, I fought the hood back down off the windshield and examined the latch. It all seemed perfectly fine. When I had checked the oil that morning and let the hood fall, its weight overcoming the power of the tired hinge springs, it had only caught the secondary latch and not the main latch. As I bounced and rocketed down the gravel road, the hood had jolted so violently that the secondary latch let go and the hood traveled back well beyond the range of the hinges only to be stopped by my windshield. The hood hinges still worked, but now they had a much greater range of motion than previously.

I closed the hood and she latched soundly. I eased on into town. From then on I followed my dad's coaching about driving downhill and followed it religiously. If I had closed the hood securely or not driven at breakneck speed, this terrifying minute would not have happened. I did not tell Don about this incident. I had not lost any wheat or permanently damaged any equipment but the incidents that Don did not know about continued to mount.

Standing on the running board one early evening in a South Dakota field, the last rays of the sun struck the cylinder of wheat streaming out of an auger. Even to a sixteen-year-old who thought mostly about homesickness, girls, football, and hunting, it looked beautiful. I was unloading on the go and watching an almost perfectly round stream of wheat flow from the auger. I was struck by the beauty of the stream enhanced by the long rays of the dropping sun. It was beautiful flowing out of the auger and beautiful sliding down the mound inside the box of my truck and beautiful at rest in this miniature mound. The gold color and the flow of it and the way the kernels slid against each other were both beautiful and fascinating. The kernels were so amazingly slippery and moved against each other effortlessly as they fell and slid and rested as near the bottom as they could reach. Even the smell was striking—musty and earthy.

From the first of the summer I had loved to watch the flow of the gold bushels coming out of the auger and mounding out in the truck. I loved the effect when I sped up to move the flow further back in the box and fill the box more evenly which caused the mound to grow like a fluid ridge in the bottom of the box and then slide down to the edges of the box and then mound up again. Then as the ridge became more of a level pile I slowed my truck again so that the auger spit the flow more to the front of the box and back and forth—speeding up and slowing down next to the steady pace of the combine. The ridge of slipping wheat from the front of the box to the back of the box and to the front again built as the little fluid ridge reached the edges of the box on each side and began to fill the box until the entire box was even full—the bouncing of the truck settling the wheat down to an almost level load and finally to a perfectly level load. Each new load from a combine—the box of the truck could take five or so hoppers from a combine—changed the dynamics of the pile and changed the feel of the truck. That night more than ever, I appreciated the beauty of the grain and had a small glimpse into the value of that grain to the people of the world.

World-wide more than twenty billion bushels are harvested every year to feed countless people. The beauty of the flowing mounding wheat in the late sun of a South Dakota afternoon becomes the beauty of nourished people around the world.

When a person walks through the bakery section of a supermarket and then through the entire store, they will see final products of wheat in countless different forms. Most shoppers do not think of the origin and the process of those many products. In truth most of us walking through the bakery are no longer even struck by the stunning variety of final wheat products. In the villages of most third world countries, the final form of the harvested wheat is in one form and is eaten in that one form every day of every lifetime—every day if they are blessed with harvested wheat.

In the bigger towns of South Dakota and the entire US the final form of processed wheat can be purchased in the following and more: white bread, wheat bread and whole wheat bread, artisan sea salt filone bread, seven grain bread, nine grain bread, twelve grain bread, English muffins, cinnamon rolls, split-top butter bread, flour tortillas, donuts of two dozen plus varieties, brownies, fruit bars, pop tarts and pretzels. Beyond all this are the millions of pounds of raw flour that people take home and transform into family recipes and potluck favorites. Whenever a person puts any one of these products in their shopping basket it is because someone somewhere on the North American continent fired up a combine and drove it around in ever shrinking rectangular shapes for hours.

Even as a teen I could see the beauty of wheat and I was then, and remain today, a "breadoholic." That summer I could have with little provocation eaten my weight in bread. Even as a sixteen-year-old with a high metabolism my weight was growing due in part to bread consumption.

As the days of summer wore on and the days in South Dakota were winding down the entire crew seemed to grow more restless. The Three Musketeers became more and more agitated. The work or the monotony or their own relationships or something was wearing on these three men and they began to party even more. Almost every night now they would take the Camaro and head for the nearest town. They partied until they ran out of money or were otherwise encouraged to leave. Invariably they would find my cot on their way into the trailer and wake me with a barrage of filthy language and detailed descriptions of their sexual conquests or fights or drinking prowess on that given night.

Even as a teen I could see a trend in their summer choices, and that trend did not lead to good places—not that they had started in a good place the day I met them only about seven weeks earlier. Their trending direction would get sad and ugly in our final stop in Shelby, Montana.

These three, and I suppose the rest of the crew, viewed me as a "goodie-goodie" who did not know how to have any fun and who was essentially wasting his summer by not going into town with them. Periodically they goaded me to join them though they knew I never would. Between my budding integrity, my well-developed sense of fear, my full blown inhibitions, and my severe reluctance to take a draw and spend money, I was never tempted to join them. Sometimes I would lay awake at night and imagine walking into a bar as a fresh-faced teenager with three hard-living men in their late thirties. My mind had few categories for where that scene would go, and the few categories it had I did not like. It was one of the few times in life when my timidity served me well.

When we finished in South Dakota toward the end of July I found a pay phone to tell my folks that we were heading on to Montana. I made some final arrangements for Dad to pick me up when the summer finished in a few weeks. Rather than have me fly home from Montana, he had decided to come get me. We worked out the day and the town where Don could leave me for the pickup and said goodbye.

As a harvest crew most of our moves had been for fairly short distances, and so far all had been far less than two hundred fifty miles. Now we were facing a drive of more than six hundred miles through some desolate sections of Eastern Montana.

As we prepared to leave my home area I thought about how much had happened and how much I had changed in a few short weeks.

Certain times in life are unusually formative and impactful. They are times when new things happen or hard things happen or strange things happen. They are times when something precious is lost or something longed-for is gained. They are times when relationships or places or occupations change—for the better or for the worse. They are times when personal support systems are removed or weakened leaving a person either alone or searching for new support.

Just as the mind is wired to pay attention to things that are close, things that are moving, things that are colorful and things that are dangerous—so the soul is wired to focus on things that are new, frightening, valuable, hurtful, helpful and unexplainable. During those times of terrific soul-alertness the mind intensely records the story we are living and is unusually efficient at retrieving the recordings. The heart is especially sensitive to injury or love or potential injury or love. The soul is awake and alive—and very soft to incoming impressions.

The summer of 1969 was one of those times for me. Much of my summer was spent in "first-time culture shock." It was the first time I was away from my parents for more than four days. It was the first time I was kissed. It was the first time I was in an auto accident, and the second. It was the first time I drank a beer, and the second. It was the first time that I was sure I was going to jail, and the second. It was the first time I had a front row seat on a horrible marriage relationship. It was the first time I saw a man near death. It was the first time I thought that I would be killed, and the second. It was the first time I experienced all these things and it was the first time I experienced anything of any magnitude where I did not have a ready, if not always happy, support system.

It was the first time that I realized the vast array of pursuits that occupied other people. I guess I knew that not everyone in South Dakota was a high school student. I am sure I didn't know that some of them were planting and fretting about wheat, some of them were repairing combines, and some of them were selling train loads of wheat to the highest bidder.

The end result of this state of soul-alertness is a layer of life sediment in my personal formation that is very distinct and very retrievable.

9 BIG SKY AND BIG DRIVE

Like so many stretches of our lives,
his plan was just to get by and wait
for the good stretch that was coming.

The move north and west from South Dakota was by far our longest haul. Between the Black Hills of South Dakota and Havre, Montana—our next destination—there was far less wheat country. Much of eastern Montana was dry-land ranching country—very arid and very big. Huge acreages were needed to run a decent number of cows. Most of the land could not be traversed by a tractor pulling a wheat drill, much less by a combine. There was also not enough water for growing wheat. But cattle could traverse the hills and gullies and they could also walk to a water tank. They did much better in most parts of eastern Montana than did wheat.

The wheat was ready in northern Montana along the Hi-Line. Don was anxious to get there.

"We're going to push hard for the next two days," was his warning at breakfast.

No one responded. No one wanted to say, "Yippee!" and no one wanted to say, "Damn it!" One was a lie and one was wasted breath. It would take two very long days to traverse the six hundred plus miles from the Black Hills to Havre.

The most northerly route of the original Great Northern Railway was only thirty miles south of the Canadian border and was called the Hi-Line. The name stuck for the railroad, but now it generally referred to US Highway 2 and the dozen or so miniature towns in northern Montana that lined that road. Don had very little acreage to cut in Havre but was optimistic about getting more.

We got an early start on our first day, and Dan was driving the first leg while I rode along in Old Red. The day became hot very quickly. With the windows down and a hot wind blowing inside we were both being dried out like jerky in a food dehydrator. The hot wind added substantially to the fatigue of wrestling the loaded truck and bouncing trailer along winding two-lane roads.

On some of the grades in Montana my old Ford, burdened with an eight thousand pound combine and trailer, would bog down to twenty miles an hour. Dan and I sat in the cab with the metal accelerator, rubber cover long since gone, mashed to the metal floor, rubber floor mat long since gone, and crawled up the hills. People in cars screamed around us, and the rest of our own trucks left us far behind. We always pulled into our prearranged stopping point well behind the caravan.

Our route took us through Spearfish, South Dakota: home of the world famous Spearfish Passion Play and the town where I had gone to grade school. Riding through Spearfish my mind was flooded with memories of four years, ages five through nine—years when my memories first began to stick. Before Spearfish, I remembered very little of my vagabond childhood. From Spearfish, I remember my first year of school, wading a creek with my brother that nearly washed us away, my first fist fight, a beautiful girl in third grade, failing spelling test after spelling test, having my football stolen, and much more. My most vivid memory was of my first epileptic spell which happened in second grade: feeling electricity run through my face and left side of my body and falling down and becoming unconscious. Then the semi-conscious ride in the back of our station wagon to the Deadwood Hospital while my mother drove faster than she had in her life. The ten days in the hospital. The multiple tests. The "I have no idea" diagnosis and the ride back home. That was the first of my seizures that mercifully ended when I was thirteen.

Spearfish was far too small to recall all that happened there—the little speed bumps in life's path that feel like earthquakes to an immature boy. Long before I could have reflected on all of it we would be out the other side of town and lumbering toward Montana.

Then to Belle Fourche, South Dakota, which I had ridden through dozens of times in the back of my parents' station wagon as we made our way to visit my grandparents in Isabel. Our caravan cut through the tiniest corner of Wyoming and into the far southeast corner of

Montana—through the towns of Alzada, Broadus, Lame Deer, Busby, Crow Agency, Hardin and then into Billings for our first night. In that southeast corner of Montana we drove across the Northern Cheyenne Indian Reservation and the Crow Indian Reservation. The country was huge, open, and brown and had plenty of relief—up and down ravines and hills. This was my first time on this road, and it was a lonely place. It was a long way between towns, at least in a crawling wheat truck.

The towns along the route were small, tired and sad. They were not like towns that had seen better days but like towns that never had better days. Most buildings were ragged and ill-kept. Cars and pickups that were no longer running sat on concrete blocks. Many homes had pretty well deteriorated to shack status. The burgs were depressing for me just to drive through—let alone live in. I loved small towns having lived in so many of them as the Forest Service pin-balled our family all over the West—South Dakota, Texas, California, South Dakota, Wyoming, Colorado and back to South Dakota. Most of our towns were little, but these towns in the corner of Montana seemed so depressed and isolated that I was glad we were just moving through.

We drove within a couple of miles of the entrance to the National Monument commemorating The Battle of the Little Bighorn, better known as Custer's Last Stand. In June of 1876 General George Armstrong Custer and the 7th Cavalry Regiment were hammered by a collection of Native American tribes including Lakota, Northern Cheyenne and Arapaho. We did not stop. I added the Custer Battlefield to the list of things that we had not stopped for—Mount Rushmore, Devil's Tower, The Badlands, Chimney Rock National Historical Site, Custer State Park and two dozen other attractions like massive balls of twine, two-headed calves, Wall Drug, The Thing, Wind Cave, The Mystery Thing, one-eyed lambs, county museums, county fairs, rodeos and carnivals. We were wheat harvesters, not tourists. Stopping was out of the question.

We had barely cleared the tiny northwestern bit of Wyoming. Dan was still driving and I was reading a copy of Sports Illustrated that I had picked up at home a few days earlier. It was the only magazine I subscribed to and I remember the pride of getting my first issue a couple of years earlier when I was a sophomore in Denver. I loved the magazine. I was a mild sports fan, but the magazine, which came to my door every week with my name on it, represented some level of adulthood to me. "I subscribe to a magazine and it comes to my house every week and it comes to me with my name on it and I must be somebody!" was my general thinking.

I was reading an article about a professional baseball player named Ken Harrelson. He had a large, hawk-like nose and was for obvious reasons nicknamed "Hawk." The article about Harrelson presented him as a good ballplayer and a very cool guy. There were pictures of the Hawk off the field, his mod dress and his mod pad.

Dan looked over at what I was reading, saw a couple of the pictures, and asked me what the article was about. I explained briefly about the Hawk, his baseball abilities and his "write my own ticket" way of life. Dan was very interested. Ken Harrelson and Dan were soul mates—free-thinking, free-dressing, free-talking and freewheeling. The one little difference was that Ken Harrelson was a professional baseball player at the top of his game and Dan was a wheatie making, at this very moment, seventy-five cents an hour for driving a two-ton truck through an Indian reservation in southeastern Montana.

Dan was so interested in the article about Ken Harrelson and had to read the article so immediately that within two minutes he said to me, "I'm sick. Something is wrong with me. I am seeing double and everything. You've gotta drive."

"Okay," I said, "pull over."

"No, I'll just climb out the door and around back to the other side," was his reply.

"Are you crazy?!"

"It's no problem. Here just take the wheel," he said to me then opened the door and started to exit. He was crazy. He was also driven by his appetites and at this instant his appetite was to read an article in Sports Illustrated. In a matter of twelve seconds he had announced that he was sick and seeing double and that I had to drive and had opened the door and begun to exit.

I took the wheel and slid over, going about fifty miles an hour, as Dan went out the driver's door. He grabbed the chain holding down the combine, pulled himself up on the bed of the truck, squeezed between the front of the combine and the back of the cab, reached down to open the passenger door, snaked around the edge of the bed and back into the cab in the passenger seat. It probably took three minutes for all this while I was driving down the road trying not to make any sudden turns, believing that Dan was going to kill himself and watching his wind-whipped shirt and hair in the rearview mirror.

When Dan got into the passenger seat, he leaned his head against the back window for maybe two minutes, then magically felt better, and picked up my Sports Illustrated and began reading about Ken Harrelson. It was the same kind of magical cure that I often felt when I told Mom I was too sick to go to school and then somehow felt good enough to go out and play when the school bus was gone.

I was glad that Dan had not died and still shocked. I was also amazed that he would have any sliver of a belief that I did not know exactly why he had done the crazy thing that he just did. The excuse for needing me to drive, the dangerous climb around the back of the cab, and the almost immediate reading of the article gave Dan no sense of foolishness or guilt. He had what he wanted and he was fine with how he got it and with whatever I thought about it. I drove the rest of the way to Billings.

Don was not going to invest the time to find a trailer park for one night and hook up the water, sewer, and electric. So he found a cheap motel in the eastern part of Billings. He and his family stayed in the motel while we slept in our trailer—meaning me on my cot—and we used the toilets in a gas station across the street. I put my cot between the shop truck and Don's pickup so as to have some privacy from the passing cars, pedestrians and street lights.

I was more and more happy to be in my cot and not in the trailer. Tonight it was not parked anywhere near to level and the smell was horrible on a hot and windless night. My cot gave me some flexibility to find level places with a little airflow and a little less odor from the bodies of seven other wheaties.

The next morning we walked to a café just a block away and had a hasty breakfast. Somewhere there is a code book, like the book for electrical codes, which defines what a café in a tired place must be like. Whoever enforces these "tired café codes" does a whale of a good job!

The code reads something like this: Linoleum-topped tables. Mismatched chairs with ripped seats. Huge, heavy white plates and coffee cups. Menus that stick to your hand when touched. Prices marked out with a magic marker and a new, higher, price written in. A serving counter with a row of stools, upholstery ripped and stuffing peeking out. Serving counter washed so many times that the color is faded. Multiple warning signs on the door designed to make you feel welcome: "No shirt, no shoes, no service!" "We reserve the right to refuse service to anyone!" "This property protected by Smith and Wesson!" "Restrooms for paying customers only!" "No Soliciting!" "No credit cards accepted!" "Local checks only!" Cash register at the front door. Toothpicks in a little shaker jar. Yellowed newspaper cartoon taped to the back of the cash register with a joke about a rancher and a banker and a bull being repossessed. Rodeo poster on the window advertising a rodeo/concert/tractor pull. Seed company calendar behind the cash register the mandatory two months behind. Syrup in an ancient sticky glass jar with a metal handle and pull back lid. Butter patties in little squares, on little cardboard squares, and covered with thin paper squares. Wire condiment holders at the end of the table with a place for napkins, salt and pepper shakers, hot sauce, catsup and sugar. Cream in a little metal pot with a flip-up metal lid. Restrooms you hold your breath in. Sticky floors of several different types of floor coverings—linoleum butted up against indoor/outdoor carpet butted up against greasy wood floors. A cardboard rack on the counter next to the cash register with copies of the owner's nephew's self-published book about growing up in Lame Deer ("There's Nothing Lame about Lame Deer"). Owner's dog lying in the highest traffic route. The "regulars" in their assigned seats eying the "not-from-around-here's" with suspicion and then sneering and then turning away to quiet ridicule with the other locals. Every conceivable make and model of waitress is allowed. Waiters are not allowed, unless you own the place. Massive meals. In any ag country café "The Rancher Breakfast," by code, must include: three eggs (as you like them), hash browns, three buttermilk pancakes, toast, bacon, sausage and coffee.

Don was in his standard "the combines are not running and I am not making any money and I am paying you yahoos" frame of mind. I ate my Rancher Breakfast so fast I felt sick.

We walked back to leave, and Don told Dan to drive the shop truck which was towing the crew trailer. I hoped he would not get double vision today because I would be in Old Red and could not take over for him.

We checked oil and gassed up and lined up to leave Billings. We had driven a matter of blocks when our caravan of metal was "cut in half" by a passing train. The first three rigs had already crossed the tracks when the lights and bell began to signal an oncoming train. Dan was just ahead of me in the shop truck. He hit his brakes and stopped short of the tracks. He had stopped short of the tracks but right under the railroad crossing arm. It came down and rested at a forty-five degree angle on the corner of the crew trailer.

I set my brake and ran up to the trailer. Dan ran back to the trailer. The arm was just perched there, but even though the shop truck was way beyond the crossing barrier it was not going to be hit by the train. We both shrugged and went back to our trucks. The whistle blared, the train passed, the arm went up and we went on.

Driving alone for the entire day, I was watching Dan weave back and forth ahead of me and watching Tim ease steadily along in my rear view mirror. In the field I had to watch for swinging augers, unload combines, leave for town, weigh and dump and weigh, drive back and watch. It was all fairly mindless, but it also broke up opportunities for long times of reflection.

Alone in the truck I had only to keep in my lane in the openness that is Montana. The mental ease of the day's driving sent me off on a journey through the summer's parade of people—a parade of the most diverse and disconnected characters imaginable.

I thought about the Fords and their kindness in putting Dan and me up overnight on our way to Oklahoma. When I lived in Denver as a junior high student, my brother and I found an old toilet and put it on the top of the Ford's chimney. We thought it was hilarious and we thought everyone else would too. The Fords thought it was offensive. We were made to go up and take it down; everyone was unhappy and Alan and I felt like both heels and martyrs. The incident did not sever our relationship with the Fords but it did create a permanent distance that was never bridged.

Then I came back through Denver a mere one year later and I was treated like a long-lost nephew. They were clearly happy to see me and they wanted to know all about my life and family since we had moved away. They fed me and gave me a house key and said, "Let yourself in whenever you get home tonight." I was glad of all of it but surprised. It was the first time I had experienced the healing that time and distance can cause—the preservation of fond affections and good memories along with the suppression of ugly and hurtful things. It surprised me, but I liked it.

I thought about the night with Carrie, Dan, and Carrie's friend at Elitche's Amusement Park. I couldn't even think of the other girl's name now or really much about her except that she felt plenty awkward that night. And she should have with Carrie and me in the back seat making out and Dan in the front seat doing drugs and talking like a big shot. I thought about Carrie and how beautiful, smart, and fun she was and about how I had been hopelessly in love with her when I lived in Denver. I thought about her having a boyfriend who was older than me and a football star and about me being a tag-along kid brother who was taller than both Carrie and her boyfriend. Now it seemed confusing to me that Carrie had been so willing to meet me in Denver, drive me around, make out with me, talk to me, hold hands with me and sit close to me in the amusement park.

Now, inexplicably, I had no romantic feelings for her and had hardly thought of her since that night and had no intentions of trying to see her again. Somehow I sensed that Carrie was less confident now and maybe less loyal too. Perhaps the pain of her broken relationship had caused some temporary or permanent harm to her psyche. Foundationally, I really liked her and admired her and thought she was beautiful. Now I was piloting an old truck down a back road in Montana and wondering why I wasn't madly in love with her. I was not.

I had a gift for falling in love with a girl in 28 minutes, and I had done that with Carrie three or so years earlier. Not this time. But I had done just that—fallen in love in eight minutes—with the quiet waitress in the late-night diner and with the quiet girl standing by the grain chute at her dad's farm. I did not know them at all but something in them hooked something in me. In the noise and confusion of my mind and heart there was something tranquil about these two girls that attracted me. Their faces were fading from me now but their spirits, which seemed nearly identical to each other, were not fading. I still sensed them in their quietness, self-confidence and contentment just moving through life with grace—both physical and spiritual. They were both so unassuming and seemed so free from any need for people to approve of the way they went about life. There was no way, short of a "Class A" miracle, that I would ever see either of them again, and I was sadder about that than about Carrie.

How do you know what attracts you to a person or a personality? How do you know what makes something not work the second time around? It was all beyond me.

My thoughts landed again on Dan. Ahead of me he must be reading something as the crew trailer and shop truck wandered freely but mostly in his lane. I had thought about Dan so much and talked to him so much and already sized him up as an insecure, big-talking pothead—a label which I now see as a horrible disservice. My approach-and-avoidance relationship with Dan also confused me. Part of me liked him, wanted to be friends at some level and wanted him to be safe despite continually dangerous choices. Part of me hated Dan because he made me so anxious and was so unpredictable. Mainly I hated Dan because of something I did not understand until decades later. Without understanding it I saw in Dan a healthy dose of my own insecurities. He dealt with his through clowning, risk, drugs, and his continual personal theater. I dealt with mine mostly through compliance and worry. His insecurity shone a bright spotlight on my insecurities.

Behind me Tim's driving was an extension of his soul—steady and quiet—an outer extension of his inner life. But that center was somehow sad. His steady and quiet center seemed more a matter of resignation than a matter of choice or confidence or contentment. Tim seemed to be a man who knew he was adrift in the world. He believed he did not have whatever it took to thrive and was quietly making the best of it. Making the best of it meant following Gary, who needed followers, and enjoying the occasional pleasures that he could glean from a beer or a woman. Tim knew perfectly when to grab some pleasure and when to "go along to get along." He was a foundationally likable man but also a man for whom I felt sad. The extrapolation of his life could not end in happy places. I thought of Tim through the lens of my own growing drivenness and ached for him.

Part of that dark future for Tim, maybe most of that dark future, was created by the arrogance, manipulation, and stupidity of his leader. Gary was in a state of great discontentment without a couple of guys following him around like puppies on a stout leash. The stout leash that drew both Kerry and Tim was really a pitifully thin leash that was braided out of a few cigarettes, a little cash, an occasional six-pack, transportation in a hot Camaro, and a senseless adventure that ricocheted back and forth in pursuit of money and pleasure. Kerry had no resources given the fact that he was the poster boy for irresponsibility even in the '60's. Tim had no resources given the fact that he had no confidence and that he was following a man no one should follow. Whatever my own assessment of the triangle of unhealthy relationships between the Three Musketeers, that triangle existed—at least for a couple of more weeks.

Gary had seen the harvest crew as a shot at some big money. He thought that he would work all summer and get a big check at the end. In the fall he was planning to live high and wild for a few weeks or months after being an indentured servant to a wheat cutter. What Gary did not foresee, though it was as clear as a red-shirt freshman telegraphing a cross-court pass, was his own decision to take constant draws against his wages all summer long. In his self-deception he did not see that he was burning through all his money almost before making it. The constant draws may have actually put Gary in debt to Don by this time in the summer. While Don could not have been happy about it he needed Gary, and all of us, so it was best to just put up with it.

Gary forged ahead. Loud-mouthed. Filthy-mouthed. Self-destructive, addicted to his desires, mostly stupidly boisterous, then, on rare occasions, funny and even endearing. I could not figure out where the line lay in his heart between real friendship with Kerry and Tim and simply needing them to affirm him—to affirm him in the face of being in his late thirties with a legacy of failed marriages, estranged kids, no education, no money, scrapes with the law and an identity defined almost solely by a Camaro.

To me Kerry was the simplest man to read, and also the most unlikable. Tim held pieces of his life that tempted you to like him or at least pity him. Kerry had none of this. He was simply mean and callous. He just felt dangerous. He was also smart. Mostly his meanness and dishonesty were enough in check to keep him from getting fired or getting beaten senseless. There was some self-preservation in his makeup but it was slight compared to his self-absorption. Kerry simply went after what he wanted with a level of guile that was repulsive. Everyone knew he was tricky and deceptive. He knew that we knew, but kept at it anyway. He was a man in a trap to his own personality and wants and style of relating. His tactics only worked sporadically but they were all he knew and he stuck with them. I never left anything of value in Kerry's presence. He was forever bumming cigarettes. His laziness caused him to become good at getting completely away from work. Drinking made him crazy wild, and he drank a lot.

Kerry's build was thin, but by this late in the summer he was to the point of looking sick. He was not "wiry" in the sense of being slight, fit and powerful. He was skinny with spindly legs and arms, and no waist or butt. I marveled all summer long that a man who was maybe five-foot nine-inches with spindly arms and weighed way less than one hundred forty, would want to be in fights all summer long. His meanness, compounded by drunkenness, betrayed him continually, and he came back to the crew trailer more than once with black eyes or open cuts or swollen lips or horrible bruises or swollen welts on his forehead, arms and back.

He had an affinity for beaten-down women. From southern Oklahoma to northern Montana, Kerry was in a string of one-night to eight-night stands with women who were thin and haggard and who wore both fatigue and despair on their faces like too much blush. They were chain smokers who tended bar or waited tables, left their kids with their grandmas and found a morsel of love of some description in serial relationships with the Kerrys of the world. One of these very tired women would occasionally show up at the crew trailer looking for Kerry or drop him off for work in the morning. Invariably their clothes were worn, their hair was unkempt, and their car was junk. The relationships between Kerry and these women were "sadness finding its own level," and it kept on all summer.

On this day, well ahead of me in the combine caravan, Mark was leading in Don's pickup pulling Don's house trailer. It was as if Mark wanted us to get to Havre as soon as possible and get to cutting. Somehow, if we got to Havre sooner, we were closer to his leaving all this behind. By now, in August, Mark was clearly a horse headed to the barn—just weeks short of his final day as a wheat harvester and just weeks short of his final year of college.

Mark had grown more distant as the summer wore on. His main goal was to get the work done with the least possible contact with anyone. He had no choice but to be in contact with Don and to manage us—but it was all done with as much physical and emotional distance as possible, and with as much economy of words as possible. He was never unkind and I did not even see him as arrogant. But there was a disdain for harvesting and for some of the harvest crew, and the boredom and the too many summers of doing this had overcome Mark. He had simply had enough. He was unwilling to quit but also unwilling to engage. Like so many stretches of our lives, his plan was just to get by and wait for the good stretch that was coming. By this time in our odyssey Mark's two main goals were to keep the sun from bleaching his thick brown hair and get done with what was, for him at least, a dragging out summer.

Each time after the occasional stops for fuel, food, and soda I went back to thinking about the crew. The one crew member I did not know how to think about was Cliff. He had the gift of contentment. Life just seemed to Cliff to be good, and it seemed to be good all the time.

Beyond that unusual skill Cliff also had the ability to be in a place, do what was expected of him, and not be noticed. Somewhere along his short seventeen years leading up to the harvest summer he might have been hurt or abandoned or belittled, and he had decided to deal with this pain through a highly perfected relational camouflage. Perhaps he was wired for quietness and contentment. Maybe he was painfully shy and afraid to truly engage. More than once during the summer I looked around the supper table and realized, "Oh, Cliff is here." He had been there the whole time but I had not noticed him. It was perplexing to me because he was not physically hiding or refusing to talk or refusing to pass the potatoes—I just never realized he was there.

In this habit of relational camouflage Cliff did not seem at all angry or unkind or manipulative. He was not trying to draw attention to himself with his quiet and withdrawn approach as many do. He just preferred to not be there among us, and when there was no choice but to be with us he had perfected the ability to not seem to be there.

The saddest member of our summer clan, even more tragic to me than any of the Musketeers, was Marie Dexter. More than any of us Marie was trapped somewhere that she did not want to be and trapped with people she did not want to be with—Don Dexter being the main source of pain in her personal cage. Marie as any woman would, hated the fears and the ongoing evidence that when she was not with him, her husband was chasing anything with a skirt. She hated the work of preparing meals for the crew three times most days. She hated the living accommodations and the moving. She hated the whining of her three children—all of whom believed themselves to be the center of the universe and bitterly resented any evidence to the contrary.

If Cliff was the most content person I had known in my short life, Marie was the most discontent. Yet in her discontent with all of life and anger toward Don in particular, she never acted on her environment beyond complaining, pouting and attacking. Marie's anger had morphed into depression with anger and the accompanying sullenness. Occasionally her deep bitterness toward Don would spill over onto one of us in the form of a direct attack. More often her vitriolic words and spirit were directed at Don and we simply got the byproducts of sullenness and silence and the clear message that everything she did for us was an oceanic imposition.

She had quickly trained all of us to get our meal and get away. We would commonly wolf down a sit-down meal and leave the trailer or grab our sandwich and cookies and eat in the shade of a distant truck—out of earshot of the station wagon and the tailgate buffet.

What none of us knew was that Marie was less than a year from her death in a traffic accident. She would leave the world at the intersection of two farm roads in the back fields of Kansas—T-boned by a truck that killed her and scattered the crew's noon meal across a quarter acre of wheat. When I learned of this terrific sadness years later, I pictured the overturned station wagon with wheels still turning, Marie's lifeless body in the stubble, pickles, Oreos, lunch meat, and chips scattered violently in wheat stubble.

It would be a sad ending to what had deteriorated to a sad life. Marie would die doing what she did not want to do for people she did not want to be with and in constant suspicion of a husband she had grown to hate. The one kindness in it all, and it was a great kindness from God, is that her children were not with her. Eventually my pity for her would morph into compassion. Whatever the ugliness and misguided nature of her own choices, Marie had a hard, sad go of things for her final years of life. How Don felt or reacted over her death I have no idea. On the one hand I imagine him feeling free to pursue other woman. On the other hand her death may have opened his eyes and his heart to what he had actually lost.

Don Dexter was in large measure culpable for Marie's hard, sad go of things at the end. Don, as I thought about him having known him now for more than two months, was set on making life good for Don. And in that pursuit he was tenacious. He chased money, women, and personal advantage—in any opportunistic order suited to a given day. Like many people afflicted with narcissism Don seemed mostly oblivious to the negative relational impact of his self-absorption. He was so much committed to himself and his own good that he did not seem to register the responses of anger or disbelief or disgust from the people whom he used. If these did register he truly did not care.

Yet Don had a compassionate element somewhere inside that would occasionally erupt through the hardened crust of his selfishness. This compassion came out when he told me not to squander my wages before the summer was over, when he laughed off my mistakes, and when he affirmed me for some act of faithfulness. At times humor would also break through to the surface—typically when he had just gotten paid for a big job, landed a big job or gotten the machines successfully loaded. For brief periods of time Don was enjoyable and those times seemed to be periods of fleeting freedom from the tyrannical god of his own happiness.

The sun was very low now, slanting at us from off to our left. We were climbing up the globe to Havre, Montana. The low-slanting rays of the dropping sun hitting the mosaic of bugs and dirt on my windshield made the driving visibility horrible. I strained to keep centered in my lane, bobbing my head back and forth between the two biggest "clean" spaces on the windshield.

And then there was me to think about. I thought about me a lot but did not think about me well. As with most teens I was too close to me for much rational thought and too ignorant of the forces outside me and the forces inside me that had shaped me and were still sculpting me: my distant, self-absorbed angry dad; my distant, relationally-camouflaged mom; my distant, struggling siblings; my hormones; my insecurity; my idealism; my ignorance about my personal giftedness and passions; moving every two to four years for my entire life; mediocre performance in everything; anxieties about my spiritual condition; horrible bondage to laziness; without an ounce of self-control; embarrassed about my big ears and short pants; afraid of girls, the dark, my dad, heights, small places, snakes, speaking in front of people, failing in school, getting hurt in sports and getting in trouble with anyone in authority.

The first conclusion I drew was that I was a mess. My second conclusion was that I had no idea what to do about it. So I did what I was so good at—I endured. I persevered alone. I didn't ask for help and I didn't confess any weakness or confusion, I didn't read anything and I didn't try new actions or new thinking—I just kept on. I was really good at enduring and passively accepting my misery and confusion. My thoughts about myself always ended in this same chaotic cul-de-sac.

There were dozens more people to think about, but I was out of emotional energy to think about anyone. I drove on in the fading light with a bug-smeared windshield and into the anxiety of dusk's low visibility where there was not enough daylight to see well and not enough dark for the bug-covered headlights to help much either. I endured.

The sun was down and everyone was bushed when we rolled into Havre. We simply parked the caravan in a long line along a side street and went to bed—everyone else in the trailers and me on my cot between my truck and the crew trailer. We would worry about a trailer park in the morning.

In the morning we did worry about a trailer park, set up, geared up and set about our routine, but we should not have. Havre was a bust on wheat cutting and making money. We got very little wheat to cut and we had more than the normal combine breakdowns. Don made a long drive to Great Falls for parts and things.

On one run to Great Falls Don took me along for reasons that were not clear to me. We rode for hours in the pickup in mostly silence. I stood with him in the parts store while he got some pulley or belt or bolts. We rode back in mostly silence for some more hours. My presence may have been simply to give Marie some assurance that he really was going for parts. If so, it meant a lot of boring hours for me. We all have ways of using each other, especially those under our control, for our own ends. I had not thought much about it, but that was probably not the only time Don used me that summer in some way. It was probably me because Marie and everyone else viewed me as a Puritan. I was someone who would look mighty nervous if I was asked to lie for Don.

The second day in Havre we began to cut on the only substantial field we had. It was going to take a day at the most. On that day, in terrific preoccupation with my ever worrying mind, I experienced my most frightening moment of the summer—more frightening than the snake or the mirror smashing or the hood plastered against the windshield event. It happened in one second and it was over the next. It may have been the world's shortest true crisis. It was for me one second of terror and disbelief.

Back in Lawton, Oklahoma, on my first day in Don's trailer, when I received my five or eight minutes of training and orientation at his breakfast table, Don had hammered three things. "First, always check your muffler for straw. Second, don't drive my trucks crazy. Third, never, ever stick your hand down in one of the augers or near the belts."

On admonition number one I was periodically guilty. I checked my muffler for straw most of the time. Not always.

On admonition number two I was mostly innocent—except for an incident rocketing down a hill on a gravel road with a hood pasted back against the windshield.

On admonition number three I was absolutely innocent. I loved my hands and arms and had great plans for them in the years and decades ahead. Don Dexter needed to give me little admonition to keep them out of an auger and away from belts.

I was driving lunch relief on one of the combines and filled the hopper on my rounds. I put my auger out to unload. When I hit the lever to empty the hopper, the auger plugged immediately. There was no real explanation as to why, but it was stuck and stuck hard. I put the rig in neutral, and without shutting her off and without thinking—fully without thinking—I reached into the auger, grabbed it and gave it a jerk. In a flash it came loose, began to turn, grabbed my sleeve and began to suck my hand and arm down. Adrenaline and terror exploded through me. Instantly, for no discernible reason other than the towering kindness of God, the machine died. Right at that moment, just sitting there idling like it could do for twenty hours non-stop, it died.

I pulled my precious hand out of the auger. I was stunned. I just sat there on the combine in utter disbelief that I had reached in there and greater disbelief that the machine had died. It was a long moment of entire disassociation, a depth of disbelief and suddenness that causes the mind to freeze and the emotions to lock up. Slowly some sense of reality crept back into my mind.

I held up my right hand, unharmed and strong, and just looked at it. For the first time in my life my right hand, the hand that contains the vast majority of my personal dexterity, felt like a great gift.

It made me so grateful for my hands. Every time I see a person with a hook instead of a hand, I remember my unthinking action to reach in an auger and the gift of a dying combine engine—the gift of my hand.

Less than a week into what was supposed to be a two- or three-week stay, we loaded up and moved one hundred miles west to Shelby. Havre was a financial setback to Don. Whenever Don spoke of the financial situation relating to Don Dexter Custom Harvesting and the profitability of the summer of 1969 in particular, he spoke of tight margins, probable loss and maybe going under. I never believed any of this. It seemed to be a ploy to make us work hard and be careful with equipment and not ask for a raise. All summer I believed, though I may have been dead wrong, that Don was making good, good money and that his talk of financial ruin was a ruse. Don did not care what I thought about his finances. Don cared if I got wheat to the elevator and got back with his truck in one piece. If I was in one piece, it was a bonus.

As the summer wore on Don struggled to keep his workers. On all the crews wheaties were lost along the way, shacked up with a waitress or too drunk to get back to work. The search for workers got more desperate. Low pay, hot days, long hours, incessant dust and an entire summer with wheat chaff in every crack of your body did not motivate men to stay on the crew.

If a man would come to work, then just come to work. There was no application, no background check, no interview and no need to see a driver's license or a social security card. Just come to work.

Don scoured the bars, cafés, flop houses and leads from other wheaties trying to find his wayward workers or the wayward workers of other crews. In the beginning of the summer he had trouble getting wheat to cut. Here in Shelby he had trouble getting sober men to cut it. Most mornings in August began with combing the trailer parks, truck stops and cheap hotels of Shelby, Montana, looking for workers.

Custom harvesting, like so much of life, is a steady fight for resources. Don spent four months fighting for wheat to cut and trailer parks to use and parts to install and farmers to pay him and wheaties to drive for him. He seemed very casual about the entire fight and was seldom ruffled. He mostly shuffled forward—both in his lazy physical walk and in his steady business pursuits. He never seemed to move very fast, but he did move continually.

10 SHELBY, MONTANA

One of the realities of all endeavors
is the terrific energy required to be diligent to the end.
We were losing that.

It is surprising how much you learn about towns—at least the smaller ones—in their cafés. The pictures on the walls, the stories on the placemats, the conversations that you overhear and the people who are clearly regulars explain the town where you have landed. The final place I landed with Don Dexter Custom Harvesting was Shelby, Montana. Our cutting around Shelby lasted more than three weeks.

In the first place where we ate in Shelby, the walls were plastered with pictures of a world championship prize fight staged in Shelby in 1922. "You cannot be serious!" I thought. They were. Shelby in 1969 was well off the prize-fighting map and well off most every other map. Not that I didn't like the town—I did—it was just small, planted in the northern prairies of Montana, distant from any large city and unknown to ninety-eight percent of the population of North America. So, for this town to be the location of a world championship boxing match nearly fifty years ago was amazing to me.

Shelby was founded in the 1890s as part of the expanding Montana-Central Railroad and was named after the railroad's general manager, Peter P. Shelby. Shelby himself felt the town would never become much. But she did make a run at becoming something early on with massive homesteading and then with the discovery of oil in 1922.

During that oil boom of the early twenties the city fathers landed on

153

the idea to attract more people and thus more money to Shelby by hosting a world championship prize fight between Jack Dempsey, the world champion, and a man named Tommy Gibbons, who was a virtually unknown but respectable journeyman boxer. This was their idea and as someone said, "There is nothing more dangerous than an idea if it's the only one you have."

The town of Shelby built an arena the size of a football stadium, fronted the entire prize money and fees to both boxers and both their managers, advertised the event nation-wide and then hosted what many boxing commentators consider to be one of the most boring matches of all time. Dempsey won after fifteen lackluster rounds on a unanimous decision. About 7,700 people paid to see the fight and another 13,000 figured out how to watch it for free from outside the stadium. In the months that followed the fight, four local banks went down for the count due to loaning the front money and never receiving anything back. It was a dismal failure in terms of boxing, in terms of money, in terms of attracting business and in terms of morale.

The end result of this sad story is Shelby's great pride for having hosted the fight. What was a dismal failure and an economic disaster in 1922 had become a claim to fame in 1969. Half a century has a way of changing perspective on many things—though Peter P. Shelby was mostly right about his town and her future.

In Shelby, Don found acres and acres of ripe wheat for us to cut. He was very happy, but another problem was rising. The problem was simply finding people to drive combines and trucks. The crew was dwindling. Crews lose men to homesickness, excessive partying, changing to other crews or scraps with the law. It is difficult to drive a combine from the city jail. It was not uncommon for a wheatie to jump to another crew for a little more money or a little nicer equipment or a little relief from crew tensions.

The Three Musketeers, still partying heavily, became even more irresponsible by the time we got to Shelby. It was a rare night when the three of them were not off bar-hopping on the main street. They came home tired. Occasionally, when they found an agreeable woman with a bed, they did not come home at all.

They had drawn about all the money that Don was going to give them and the tedious work of wheat harvesting had worn thin with all three of them. They were a long ways from Oklahoma and, it seemed to me, feeling very lost. Between the three of them they did not have enough gas money to get out of Montana, let alone back to Oklahoma. They missed work, came late to work, and even left early at times.

Gary had a found a woman in a bar who invited him over for one night and then two, and then he started living with her full time. He still came to work but seldom on time and seldom in any shape to work productively. Two states earlier Don would have fired him for this behavior, but here in Shelby he needed anyone with a pulse. Don tolerated the mess and the partying continued.

As the crew was slowly drifting off—tired of the work and finding more interesting "occupations" in town—I found myself driving a combine more and more. I was often cutting wheat, unloading into my truck and then, when the truck was full, driving it to town myself. On more than one day I became a one-man harvest crew with one combine and one truck while the rest of the men and machines were being one-man crews in other fields. It felt good to be a one-man harvest crew. I was proud of myself. Ten weeks earlier I did not know how to shift a split axle transmission, and now I was driving both the combine and the truck all day long without an ounce of supervision.

We cut late most nights in the Shelby area—sometimes real late. The wheat was staying dry long enough that many nights we did not shut off the machines and tarp the loads until one or two in the morning.

Don came by to check on me one night near midnight and found the moisture content was still low. We stood in the darkness and the stubble for a couple of minutes nearly shouting to each other over the noise of my idling combine. He told me to go ahead and cut for another hour. I climbed back on the open machine—I did not rate a cab to shelter me from the dust and noise—and turned to my right as his pickup lights disappeared down the road.

I was generally spooked when cutting by myself at night. This edginess was certainly the leftover dregs of my childhood fear of the boogie man in the closet. We had never had any trouble with anyone or anything in the night, or in the daytime for that matter, in any of our fields. The only troubles in our fields were self-inflicted. All the same I was spooked.

Riding along in the middle of the night the only thing I could hear was the din of the mechanical thrashing happening underneath me. And the only thing I could see was the small arena of standing wheat which my headlights illuminated in front of the header and the dancing shadows of the lights to the side as they were hitting the moving wheat. This arena of bright light was a semicircle that was only twenty or twenty-five feet across. Everything else was dancing shadows on moving wheat or just blackness.

If my eyes had a chance to adjust to the darkness I could probably see more out to the sides of my machine. But they never had that chance because I was constantly watching the wheat ahead of me so I could cut the maximum swath without missing any wheat, adjust the header if needed and turn to the right at the right time. My eyes were dilated just right for the little moving bright area of light that the combine lights created and that moved faithfully ahead of me.

In situations of darkness and anxiety, which I experienced often, I used my hearing to give myself some level of peace about my surroundings. In the din of a running combine there was no comfort from listening.

The experience of night driving became even more surreal because the incessant turning of the header fan and the motion of the mower bar and the field passing slowly under me all contributed to a mesmerizing motion. It was noisy and bright in one little place, dancing shadows on the edges, dark all around and moving and noisy and moving and dancing shadows—a 3D movie that I didn't like but could not leave.

Some minutes after Don drove off, I heard a loud and frightening noise off to my left. It was like a scream in some ways but did not sound human in other ways. It was sudden, loud, close, and shrill. It terrorized me, and instinctively I jerked my head to the left to see if I could see anything. I jerked my head with such force that I threw my black frame glasses completely off my head and out into the Montana darkness. I fought back full panic. A horrible half-human, half-animal noise had come out of the darkness in the middle of the night while I was by myself in the middle of a wheat field at least five miles from another human being and now my precious glasses—which I needed desperately for any decent sight—had flown into the back stubble somewhere.

I stabbed the clutch and the brake and brought the combine to a bouncing stop. I turned off the motor and listened for rustling, talking or the noise again, straining like my welfare depended on hearing something. There was nothing. There was only middle of the night Big Sky quiet. I looked up at the blackness and with my horrible eyesight and without my glasses could not even make out the stars.

I had no flashlight, and I dared not turn the combine around to use the lights for fear I would drive over my glasses. I climbed down the ladder in the dark and stepped onto the stubble beside the machine. Trying to gauge how far I had driven after throwing my glasses into the dark, I pointed myself in that direction and began crawling forward on my hands and knees. I was feeling ahead of myself in the dirt and stubble in hopes both of finding my glasses and of not kneeling on them in my search for them. Within five feet my hands were filthy. The first pass was unsuccessful. When I decided that they could not possibly have gone any farther, I turned around to get a view of the parked combine, moved over a swath and started crawling back. Like a very blind and inefficient combine, I combed the stubble—swath by swath—in the area where I thought the glasses should be. I searched in the dark with no certainty that I was in the area of my tossed and lost glasses and with no assurance that each pass was covering the entire area—I may have been missing wide swaths of stubble.

My despair was growing and I began to debate how long to keep up my nocturnal hands-and-knees search.

Periodically I stopped, straightened up on my knees, and listened. Nothing. I turned and looked in a three-sixty. My eyes were better adjusted to the dark though miserably poor without my glasses. Nothing. Search. Nothing. Listen. Nothing. Move over two feet. Take another swath. Nothing.

After thirty or more minutes on my knees, to my great joy, I found them! My hand hit the plastic needle in a stubble field! A pair of black glasses lay unharmed in a stubble field!

I was the happiest teenager on the planet—perhaps the happiest human on the planet.

I got on my machine, fired it up, cut a couple more rounds and called it good. I was in one of my moods where everything spooked and frightened me. I shut down the combine by the truck, ran to my truck—anxious that someone was under the truck or behind the truck or maybe even in the truck. Locked both doors fired the engine and eased happily out of the field. My old rig was safe and the doors were locked and I had my glasses and I was moving away from whatever werewolf had screamed at me in the night. It was a happy drive to Shelby and even my cot in the open air felt safe by comparison that night. Even though by now there were empty beds in the crew trailer, I never moved in—out under the stars felt far cleaner and smelled far better. And, truth be told, sleeping outside may have been a statement of separation from the crew in my subconsciousness.

As the August days wore on in Shelby, wheaties became harder and harder to find. Only one of the Three Musketeers, Tim, was showing up on a regular basis. Gary and Kerry missed many days until Kerry did not show up at all.

Most mornings began with breakfast in a café followed by a search for shacked-up workers. Don, Dan and I would get in Don's pickup and follow tips from waitresses and locals who had seen our workers.

We drove from trailer park to apartment building to back-street rental homes knocking on doors and looking for our guys.

At first Don did the dirty work while Dan and I sat in the truck. Then he began to pull up with the passenger side toward the place and say, "Just run up to the door and see if Kerry or Gary is there."

Like a child who had just been given the dirtiest chore in the house, maybe toilet cleaning, I would go up to the door and give it a gentle knock. No answer. Knock again. No answer.

"Hell, knock louder!" Don would shout from the truck. I would knock louder.

Finally someone would come to the door and it was usually someone who had been up until three in the morning either waiting on customers at a bar or being a customer at a bar. The person would either be an angry, tattooed, bed-headed ruffian who looked like he could crush my head or an angry, sleepy, bed-headed barmaid who looked like she could whip me in a fair fight. They were not pleasant encounters.

"Is Gary or Kerry here?" I would say. If it was one of the bed-headed ruffians he would say, "I have no idea who the hell that is and don't ever knock on my damn door again!" The door would slam in my face, and I would go gratefully back to the truck.

If it was one of the bed-headed women who came to the door, she would say, "I haven't seen either one of them," and shut the door in my face. They were always horrible liars. I would go gratefully back to the truck knowing full well that one or both of them was in bed in that very trailer.

On one occasion Don got a hot lead on Kerry's whereabouts and I did hit the right trailer. A bed-headed woman came to the door. She was maybe thirty-eight or forty but looked like a tired fifty-five. Her hair was a tangled mess and her robe was filthy. The trailer's living room behind her was squalor. "I am looking for Kerry," I said in my most gracious tone.

"He ain't here." was her immediate response. I stood there a moment knowing that he was there since she knew him and since our lead was a good one. "Dammit he ain't here!" she said again. I hesitated again but did not know what to say.

For some reason Kerry shouted to me from the very living room, "Gibson, you tell Dexter that I am done working for him! You tell him to never come looking for me again! To hell with all of you!" I leaned to my right and looked further into the living room to see Kerry sitting up in a sofa sleeper—he was bare chested and mercifully covered with a sheet from his waist down.

"Sure," was all that I said before I went gratefully back to the truck. I told Don. We went out to the field shorthanded.

Among the crew, and even with Don himself, our work became more ragged and less diligent. My first day back in southern Oklahoma began with a stern lecture about how to take care of equipment, how not to start a fire and how not to get hurt or hurt anyone. In the early summer the crew carefully checked zerks and oil and mufflers for straw—most of the time. We made a decent effort to take care of the machines and to keep the people safe.

For some reason, maybe fatigue or maybe a familiarity that was breeding contempt or maybe end of the season fever, that care was clearly waning. For one thing we were working more alone now and no one was there to see if equipment was being greased or not. For another thing we were short on workers. Doing the same work with fewer people left less time for maintenance and for general caution. And, when you are the only combine in a field, there is only one other vehicle to avoid hitting and that is your own truck.

Even Don was slipping in his care. One afternoon, moving between fields, I was in the pickup with Don as we pulled a header to the new place. It was a long drive and Don was in a hurry though the combine was being ferried under its own power and would not be here for a long time.

We drove along the lonely gravel road not speaking. I was staring mindlessly out the passenger side window taking in the flat wheat country when Don said, very casually, "Damn, our header is passing us."

I looked to the left and it was indeed passing us. The trailer had come off the pickup, pulled alongside us and made an attempt to pass us. The trailer veered off into the left side ditch and came to a dirt-spewing stop—tongue buried in dirt but nothing harmed.

We pulled over, backed up, cleaned the dirt out of the hitch, and hooked up again. We drove on again, this time with the latch locked and the break-away chains in place and never said another word about it. Something in Don had changed. Either he was too tired to care or he was depressed about the state of his crew or his marriage or he missed his kids. Maybe all of this. That incident clarified for me something I had seen but not fully grasped: Don had grown very sad. He was the type of man who would not tell anyone that he was sad or why he was sad. I was too young to even think of asking him.

One of the realities of all endeavors is the terrific energy required to be diligent at the end. We were losing that.

Soon after we reached Shelby, Marie had taken the kids and gone back to Oklahoma to get ready for school. She seemed very happy the day she left. It seemed strange to have them gone even though I had almost no relationship and almost no affinity for any of them. She did not bother with goodbyes to any of the crew but just loaded her kids and her things in the station wagon and drove away. How she had said goodbye to Don we did not know. Don gave no indication of how their separation had gone.

Dan had also had enough. Just as he had claimed double vision in order to stop driving our truck he suddenly concocted a reason for leaving early. One day he was his regular steady self on the combine seat and the next day he was announcing his departure. The next day he left hitch-hiking back to Rapid City. His leaving was like Marie's—quick and quiet, like slipping out a back door when you do not want to be noticed.

These departures left me with the sad feeling of being the last one at a party. I would have liked to leave but had some more days until my Dad was due to take me home. Feelings of abandonment stirred up in me dredging up childhood pains that I did not understand. I had to keep on—I had no ride home and too much rule-keeping compliance to even think of leaving early.

With Marie's departure we were now eating breakfast and supper in cafés and lunch out of bags. Don would buy an array of hastily selected lunch items and we would make our own lunch before breakfast. The meals were definitely deteriorating from the days when Marie had been with us.

When we ate in cafés, Don was on the constant lookout for drivers. He was hiring anyone. No questions asked. No driver's license needed. References would have been a joke. If a person could fog a mirror and would come that day, they were put in the truck and taken to the field.

One morning he approached a twenty-ish looking kid about working. It turned out that he was available, so he came to work for us that very day. The kid Don hired in the café that morning was named Robert. He was alone in the world since his family had some while back abandoned him and scattered. He thought he knew where his mom was, had not seen his dad in years and did not care where his half-siblings might be.

The very first day we hired Robert, he declared to the crew, without provocation and for no reason that we could figure, "I have the hottest car in town and if any cop ever stops me I will kill the bastard!" I looked at him in disbelief. What kind of a person would kill a human being over a traffic stop? Apparently Robert was that kind of person, or he wanted us to believe that he was.

He drove a very hot GTO with very loud pipes. The car was his source of pride and his only companion in life. The car was something he owned and could keep from abandoning him. It was for him a small consolation prize in a life that had taken the real prizes out of his life. As such Robert extended great care and value to the car.

His greatest personal joy was to race over the railroad overpass in the center of Shelby and, right at the top of the overpass, back off the gas pedal, creating a thundering noise with his exhaust pipes. It could be heard all over the small town.

One night a few days after Robert joined the crew I was in his car once when he crossed the railroad overpass and created the terrific noise—seemingly reverberating all across the small plains town. "I hope a cop stops us," was Robert's comment as the noise died away. "You don't mean that, do you?" was my response. "I do!" he exclaimed, "I won't take any crap from anyone—not even a cop!"

From there we rode on in silence. Robert thinking about his loneliness and abandonment and me thinking about my anxiety at being in the car with a kid who said he would kill a cop.

The thundering noise of those pipes was Robert's screaming message to Shelby and the world, "I am here and I matter." At that point Robert did not believe the message and clearly Shelby did not either.

Surprisingly Robert stayed with us. He kept himself well outside any friendship or camaraderie of the crew but still came to work. His bravado continued, but from time to time there was a small hint that Robert was glad to be part of some "family" of people who had something in common even if it was only cutting wheat together on the northern plains of Montana. It may have been the closest thing to family he had experienced for years—maybe ever.

Robert was frightening—not just to me but to the whole crew. He was frightening for his large anger and even larger insecurity which both seeped out at every little thing. He shouted, cussed, and threatened—but while I was still on the crew, he never did bite. He was a sad combination of insecurity, pain, and bravado.

Soon after Robert started, one of the deep sadnesses of that summer hit—an angry rift between Kerry and Gary. I did not learn about this until after my cussing-out by Kerry at the trailer park. All summer I got along with all the Musketeers and stayed out of their way. They mostly ignored me. Still the devastation of their friendship triangle was a sad thing to see. I am not sure why I cared about this friendship between these three as I did not respect any of them. The destruction happened after more than twenty years of friendship, and it happened over a woman who would be done with both of them in a matter of weeks or months at best.

Tim said to Don, in my presence, "The woman Gary has been with has moved on to Kerry." Tim relayed this with a matter-of-factness that thinly veiled his own sadness. Not that Tim cared who she was with but only that she had caused a rift in a friendship that he did care about. The woman in question was the tired woman whom I had encountered at the door of the trailer house the morning before. She was a barmaid at one of their favorite bars.

"She never said anything to Gary. Just invited Kerry over one night when her shift ended," Tim went on to report. "What the hell for?" was Don's question. "Hell if I know," said Tim.

Gary of course found out about Kerry and "his" girl. The ensuing confrontation came to blows. These two men who had been fighting shoulder to shoulder against others for two decades were now landing fists on each other. It was not clear who won the fist fight—the outcome of that was about as disappointing as the Dempsey-Gibbons fight fifty years earlier. However, the woman stayed with Kerry. Kerry never came back to work and we never saw him around Shelby. Don certainly did not owe him much if any money for all the draws he had taken.

Gary went home not having enough gas money to get there. He declared to Tim that he was going to work his way there. He just drove away in his Camaro and never settled up with Don.

Tim stayed on with the crew but his sadness dipped to new lows. He related to no one and quietly did his job. He was a follower and for the first time in two decades he was without a leader. His next move was very unclear so he kept to the path he was on—harvest wheat and keep moving north with the crew.

The trio had shattered and the three men were done with each other. They could never have seen it coming, but that twenty plus years of camaraderie came apart in Shelby, Montana, over a woman who bounced from man to man.

Besides the Dempsey-Gibbons fight Shelby had another claim to fame. This second claim was about as ignoble as the fight. Shelby had a whore house. Everyone in town knew about it. The establishment did not have an ad on the placemat in the local cafés with the car dealerships, insurance agencies and the auction barns, but they did have plenty of word of mouth advertising and plenty of loyal customers.

The building was a huge, converted two story farm-looking house and it was pretty much by itself on the edge of town. It had a long driveway and some acres with it.

In Montana, prostitution was both illegal and lucrative. And, in Montana and most places in the United States, it was apparently also overlooked by the local law enforcement. Perhaps the law received money for their silence or maybe even received "services" for their silence. Maybe they got nothing but the satisfaction of making sex available to the hardworking men of Shelby, Montana. Whatever the case they were silent.

Any wheatie who had been in town two days would know about it. Everyone with a longer residency than me must have known also.

Various crew members talked about the place from time to time. Some visited. It was a fall back option when they could not pick up a woman in the bar. Don knew about it but made no indication that he had ever been there.

One day as Don and I drove past it on the way to the field he said to me, "Did you ever get up to the whore house?"

"No I didn't." was my reply.

"That's too bad," he said.

I didn't know what to say. Neither did Don. We drove on in one of those awkward silences that ten years later I would have known how to break.

I had enough integrity, or maybe only enough inhibition, to stay away from "up there." I did not yet have enough integrity to report two bent pulleys to my boss.

On one of our typical late nights of cutting we shut down about one in the morning, parked the machines, and piled into the rigs that were going to town—Don's pickup, the shop truck and a two-ton.

Our trailers were parked in the middle of Shelby, and we were cutting at least twenty miles south of town. On the dirt roads in the dark with multiple turns the drive lasted a half hour. This night I was in the shotgun seat of Don's pickup and Cliff was in the middle while Don drove. Cliff and I were exhausted and dozed off and on—our heads bobbing up and down as we dropped off in fatigue and then woke ourselves with the sudden fall of our heads and jerk of our necks. We got right to the edge of Shelby and were caught by a very long freight train. The crossing arm was down, the lights were flashing and the train was creeping to the west—barely moving. We were less than a mile from our beds.

Don cussed and put the truck in park without shutting it off and leaned his head against the back window. Cliff was mostly gone.

Behind us the shop truck and the two-ton pulled to a stop and sat there, like us, with engines running and wheaties dozing. Don's headlights were on, and he was immediately asleep against his window.

I leaned my head against the passenger side window and dozed off again. The window was cold and I was horrible at sleeping while sitting up, but I was tired enough to sleep a little. The train was very long and hardly moving. Periodically I would wake up—it might have been every two minutes or every ten minutes, I had no way of knowing—lift my head, see that the train was still there and try to sleep again.

On one of those short windows of consciousness, I lifted my head and the train was still there. Centered exactly in the Don's headlights was a flat car with a tractor chained down on it. Just as that flat car and tractor traveled slowly through the beam of the pickup's lights, a bum threw a bag under the tractor and crawled up on the flat car. I just saw him inching himself under the tractor as the flat car left the arch of the headlights. Another car was now visible and the flatcar, the tractor, the bum and his bag had disappeared into the blackness.

I was the only one awake and the only one who saw him, and I have never forgotten him. I saw him for only a matter of seconds. There was no way to make out his features or his age. He just jumped up on the flatcar after his bag, edged under the tractor and was gone.

I sat there, now wide awake, staring at the train edging west and wondered about him. Wondered why he was riding trains, where he was from, if he had family and what had gone on in his life. What choices had brought him to the outskirts of Shelby on an August night with his belongings in a bag and his only means of transportation an open flatcar through the Montana night?

It is easy for me to call up the black and white mental picture of the tractor on a flat car framed in a set of headlights and the bum swinging his bag up first and then himself and then inching under the tractor. His duffle bag looked like mine.

For some reason the man mattered to me and I wondered what would happened to him.

I had just two more days of cutting with Don before I would be heading back to school in Rapid City. After I was gone, Don and the remnant of his crew moved north into Canada. From Shelby it was just thirty-six miles due north to the town of Sweetgrass on the border of Canada, Alberta to be exact, and the border of much more wheat as well. Don would leave behind a couple of combines owing to his dwindling crew.

I could not imagine going on. I was ready to be done. For me the great adventure of "travel required" was winding down. The season of excited launching was long past. The season of "this is good" break-in was long gone. The season of "I've got to keep going because there is a long time left" was now past. The season of "almost to the end" was even past. Now I was in the "all over but the shouting" phase of my adventure. I was ready to be done.

It was one of those classic winding down times when lots of folks have already left the party, the time is late, the fun is over, others are drifting off, and it feels sad to be ending but it feels about time to drift off too. The end of my employment with Don Dexter Custom Harvesting was one of those strange endings that I longed for and thought would never come. But it did come and then I felt glad it was over but also a bit sad.

Jostling along in Don's pickup into Shelby for my last midnight ride, I thought about the fact that the group of people who had started in Fort Sill three months ago would never be together again. I thought that I should not have wasted so much emotional energy worrying about my duffle bag and my gear and my time sheet and whether or not to buy cowboy boots—I never did—and what some sleepy drunk was going to say to me at the door of a trailer house. I felt sadness at leaving the crew and actually sadness toward the people who had already left— Marie, the kids, Dan and even Kerry and Gary—people I was not close to yet people with whom I had shared a very unique summer.

On the day I was leaving, Don called me into the living room of his trailer to settle up on money. He gave me a check for $750 and explained the hours I had worked both moving machinery and cutting wheat and the two draws that I had taken for $20. He had a detailed record laid out for each day and each place. I did not quite have $750 worth of time, but Don gave me a bonus of $50 for my work that summer. He said that he appreciated my hustle and steadiness.

My agony over not keeping a timesheet seemed pretty much wasted emotional energy. Don had a detailed record of our time for cutting and moving. That said, the details may have been cooked in his favor by a few hours here or there. To me he seemed honest about the whole deal. At this point it did not matter. I had never seen $750 in my entire life and it felt good. It was a lot of money to me. If Don took me for $400 that day, I never knew it and never missed it. In my bent to give people the benefit of the doubt, I don't think he did.

I thanked Don, shook his hand, and turned to walk out the door.

Don stopped me and said, "I was serious about turning her over to you next year." It was his way of saying, "I would really like to have you back next summer."

I was grateful for his affirmation and said, "Thank you. I'll be ready."

I was sixteen and had never been away from home for more than four days at 4H camp. Up until that summer I had never been on an airplane or a public bus. I had never driven a combine or a two-ton truck.

I traveled with a crew of wheaties for fifteen hundred miles through five states in twelve weeks. I ruined one mirror and one set of combine belts, bent two pulleys, got in one truck wreck, peeled back one hood flat against the windshield and creased a couple of fenders here and there. I drank a six pack of beer in one night. I avoided doing time for underage drinking. I avoided doing time in Dodge City for pool hopping. I avoided getting bitten by a rattlesnake. I avoided losing my hand in an auger. I avoided the whore house in Shelby. I avoided getting beaten up by a bed-headed ruffian. I got a $50 bonus for my efforts and came home with my duffle bag, $750, and both of my hands.

I also headed home a different person. The people and events of that summer had put me in personal transformation overdrive. I lost some naiveté and gained some courage. I gained some perseverance and lost some innocence. I gained some perspective on the world outside the confines of my sheltered family.

I concluded that the summer should go in the win column.

Though I did not realize it at the time, I had ended up being the leader of everything I had joined since I was in the seventh grade. I had not joined anything very big or noble. I had not, from what I could see, accomplished much if anything as a leader. But for reasons I could not see others, like Don, perceived me as a leader. At times I wonder how I would have done if I had gone back.

I really planned to be there again and I was almost gleeful about the prospect of being the crew foreman and getting the plush jobs. I had not intentionally lied to Don, but I never went back.

As with so much of life a great deal had changed nine months later when it would have been time to fly to Oklahoma. I could not know at the time, but I would be moving to Arizona and looking for other work and having not a shred of interest of going back to cut wheat with Don.

I never regretted not returning. At times I have wondered about what it would be like to be there when Marie died. I have wondered what it would be like to be crew foreman. I have wondered what it would be like to see the quiet girl at her dad's farm again. I have wondered what it would be like to direct six or eight wheaties—most of whom would be older than me and some twice as old as me.

Tomorrow I would leave the crew and Shelby and custom harvesting for good. Tomorrow I would be heading back to my other life—the life that was the most definite but at the moment seemed like a faded dream.

11 THE LANDING

I regretted how anxious
I had chosen to be all summer
as I spun myself up about almost everything.

My senior year would start within days. Football practice was already going. I was late getting my senior picture done. Registration had already happened for school.

My Dad had decided to drive to Montana to get me and then combine the trip home with a canoe trip. The plan was for Dad, my brother Al, and my Dad's friend Chuck Stevens to pick me up so that the four of us could go canoeing on the Big Horn Reservoir in northern Wyoming. Don agreed to take me one hundred miles to the little town of Belt in order to reduce my Dad's trip from our home in Nemo. We were both supposed to be at the agreed-upon corner at 2:00 PM.

I got up early on my final day, stuffed everything I had in my trusty duffle bag and broke down my cot for the final time. I stashed it under a bunk in a trailer without asking Don what to do with it. He didn't care, and now I didn't either.

I joined what remained of our crew for breakfast at the café with the history of Shelby littered on the walls. No one said much. I was yet another departure in a dwindling crew, and the morale of those who remained was bottoming out. I ate my last meal on Don's dime, said goodbye to the crew with a handshake and a "good luck." It was not much of a parting—I was plenty nostalgic about the summer, but no one was much attached to me.

I climbed in the passenger side of Don's red pickup, and the familiar streets of Shelby gave way to the long, lonely stretches of Montana highway.

The drive to Belt was long and mostly silent for Don and me. There was not much to talk about between a sixteen-year-old wheatie and his thirty-eight-year-old boss. Despite working together for three months, there was little common ground and we were neither one very skilled in conversation—Don because he didn't have a whole lot to say and me because I was too shy to initiate much. Don and I made the agreed-upon corner in Belt only a few minutes late. To my disappointment, Dad was not there. By 2:30PM there was no sign of my Dad, but Don said he had to go. We shook hands and said some vague things about next summer. Don drove away in his red Ford pickup.

It was the last time I saw Don Dexter. Thirty years later, assuming he was still alive, I searched for him but without success. I had, in the category of "it's a small world," run into someone from Don's hometown who knew him. They said he was living in some other city in Oklahoma and was completely out of the farming and custom harvesting business. My contact said he was selling used cars and still ran his own lot. I never found him. At the time I was looking, if he was still alive, he would have been in his mid- to late-seventies.

I want to believe that Don would remember me, but out of the eighty to a hundred-fifty wheaties who worked for Don over the years, I doubt if I lodged in his long-term memory.

I spent the next three hours pacing the street in downtown Belt and checking other corners and worrying. I kept my duffle bag on my shoulder or within sight. With my skill for creating the worst case scenario, I imagined that Dad would not find me, leaving me to sleep in the post office overnight—or maybe in jail. With my gift for anxiety I made the three hours of waiting seem like a week. I had no cash to buy a meal or a soda. I had a check for $750 that was not useful in Belt. All I could do was wander around in the sun and worry and sit on the curb.

About 6:00 PM they arrived. Dad simply said, "This burg is farther than I thought. Are you ready to go camping?" It was Dad's version of an apology and within ten minutes he had forgotten the entire situation. I was relieved and threw my gear in the back of the station wagon.

Dad treated this late arrival as if he had been ten minutes late to get me from football practice. My anger and anxiety melted away and I said nothing about my angst.

I spent the next three days canoeing, camping, and fishing with Dad, Al, and Dad's friend Chuck. Dad and I were in one canoe while Al was in the other with Chuck. From the first launch Al and I were racing. With Herculean effort I could hold my own against him—but not beat him. Al, like me, was competitive and would not slow down. I am sure my father and Chuck grinned at each other all day long as they were pulled along by two competitive young bucks. Al would go on to be a two-time state high school wrestling champion and a scholarship wrestler in college. He gained most of the strength for those accomplishments in those three days of canoe racing with me. My arms ached and felt like ribbons as the lactic acid built up and wouldn't leave. All this effort to not be shown up by my younger brother.

Mostly I had slipped into a stupor. It was an experiential whiplash in which the past three months—which had been so real and so formative and had seemed so long—were already gone. I was back in the company of people I knew and back in the practice of things I had done—canoeing and camping and fishing. Though I did not understand the concept at the time, it was a mild case of culture shock. For most of the camping trip I was thinking about the summer, the crew, the time, and all that had imprinted on me. It occurred to me that most of the time I was anxious for the summer to be over because of my severe homesickness. Now I was sad that it was over because the adventure was done. Now I also regretted how anxious I had chosen to be all summer as I spun myself up about almost everything. It had all turned out fine. I felt foolish. At least no one knew.

Our canoe trip was mostly uneventful. Dad and Chuck talked. Alan and I paddled. We all ate and slept. When we got back to our cars we said goodbye to Chuck and loaded the canoe. Even though I had been driving a truck all summer my dad was not keen on me driving. So, in boredom and my great uneasiness normally felt around dad, I slept most of the way home.

I got up the first morning I was home and drove the twenty-plus miles into town to see the football coach. Practice had already begun but he knew I was going to be late. I was still wearing my mop of white hair and Coach Egan grinned at me when I came into his office. He grinned because of his gleeful understanding that it would have to go. He was a short man, maybe five-foot and six inches, but very powerful. Besides being powerful he was willful. Despite his miniature size for a football player he had played successfully in some small college somewhere. He simply determined to have his own way in everything. Even though I was six-feet and three inches he scared the daylights out of me. He was stern, strong, and ruthless and could be mean when he was having a bad day. He was a no-nonsense man and winning was the only thing to him. Losing made him angry. If I or any player contributed to a losing effort he would vent his anger on us. He had great self-control for personal fitness and for detailed coaching of football. He had almost no self-control for his emotions.

He greeted me warmly enough and said, "You look like you are in good shape."

"I don't know," I said. Actually I did know. I was in horrible shape. I had not been running at all, was a bit overweight, had mostly been glued to the vinyl seat of my Ford for the summer. When I was not glued to the seat of my truck I was glued to a booth in some greasy spoon eating cheeseburgers, reading town histories on placemats and making eyes at quiet waitresses. I was in horrible shape and knew it and was afraid about it. Just how badly out of shape would be evident tomorrow—more to me than to him. It was another instance where I failed to prepare for something that I knew was coming and therefore was in a lot of pain when that something actually arrived.

"You're late for the season," was his next message even though he knew I was going to be late.

I was apologetic and said, "I'm sorry, Coach, but I am getting my senior picture taken today and my hair cut this afternoon and I will be out to practice tomorrow."

He grinned again and said, "I was gonna tell you that hair had to go."

"I know that, Coach," I said.

"Well go get your equipment and your locker and be here at eight tomorrow morning, suited up and on the bus."

"Yes sir," I said and walked out to find the equipment manager. It was the last "cordial" conversation I would have with the man until I accidentally ran into him in a store thirty years later. The rest of the season he would mostly be screaming at me, questioning my heritage, and instructing me, oftentimes with his hand wrapped around my facemask and my head pulled down to his level.

I wore a hideous brown suit to my senior picture and grinned at the camera—black-rimmed glasses, mop of white hair, baby face and big ears. The picture still hangs in the sewing room of my parents' home next to the hideous pictures of my four siblings. At the time it seemed like a pretty sharp picture. Today the five pictures together look like a freak show.

From the studio I was off to the barber for my scalping. The barber took great delight in removing my shaggy hair down to "football length" which was about a quarter of an inch. He not only ribbed me the whole time but joked with the other barbers and customers about the process. When he spun me around and gave me my glasses, I was a different kid. Now I had a white head instead of white hair and my already huge ears looked like they had grown during the summer growing season.

The next morning at eight I was suited up and on the bus. As a senior I was attending a brand new school—open for the very first year—and without our own football field as yet. Our practices took place at a public park some miles from the school so we would suit up at the school and ride the bus to and from practice.

My first day of practice was more brutal that I anticipated—and I was anticipating a lot. I was in the horrible physical condition that I believed I was in. Shifting an old split axle Ford is tricky, but not aerobic.

We practiced twice a day for the first two weeks—until school started. "Two-a-days" have been dreaded by about every football player on the planet. Conditioning and basic football skills—mostly conditioning— were the focus of those two weeks. I was so exhausted after morning practice that I went to Dan's house near the school and slept until he woke me up to go to afternoon practice. Dan was sleeping most of the day, doing drugs, and being kind to me. We had experienced an adventure together that gave us some bond. We both thought it might make us into friends. It did not. After two-a-days Dan and I seldom saw each other at school. When we did cross paths we said "Hi" and continued on our separate ways.

As the morning practice ended Coach Egan called the team together and said, "Two guys got to practice late this year and they are going to run an 880 against each other to pay for that."

"Crap!" I thought to myself. It was clear that I was one of the guys about to be subjected to more pain and that pain in front of the entire team. The other kid was a lanky junior whom I did not know, but he was clearly a faster runner than me. Everyone, except a two hundred forty pound sophomore lineman, was faster than me. We took off our helmets and shoulder pads and went to the starting line. Coach Egan whistled for us to go. I took off in the lead and held the lead, in searing pain and mental determination, for the first 870 yards. The junior hung behind me about three feet for that whole distance. At the end I was sprinting with all I had to win, but he came around me with ease and won the race. I regret not tackling him as he went by. I was a senior and soon to be the starting tight end and I had been easily outrun by a junior. The competitor in me resented that. Everyone on the field, from coaches to players to equipment managers, knew he was going to beat me.

That afternoon the basic skills practice and the conditioning continued with a vengeance. It was in the mid-90s and miserable. We were given salt tablets and periodic water breaks, but not nearly enough. I had a headache and about as much energy as a ninety-year-old with the flu.

The day ended with an infinite number of a hundred yard dash wind sprints. We ran in two separate groups. The backs and ends ran first and then the lineman ran next. I was a tight end and so ran with the fastest kids. I was dead last every time.

"Backs and ends on the goal line!' Coach Eagan would shout. The shrill of the whistle would release us to sprint one hundred yards—legs full of lactic acid, lungs searing, hearts hammering, and minds saying, "This is brutal. When the hell will this stop?"

I was sure every sprint was the very last. I was wrong a lot.

"Backs and ends on the goal line!"

I thought, "You cannot be serious! You are going to kill us. You are literally going to kill us." Other kids were mumbling far worse things under their breath. Occasionally, Coach Egan would hear a kid mumbling under his breath and then torture him with some special form of pain like an extra sprint at the end or 25 pushups.

Again, the shrill whistle.

For the rest of my life that sentence followed by that whistle was imprinted in my memory.

"Backs and ends on the goal line!" Shrill whistle.

When that afternoon finally ended, we filled our helmets with ice chips that the trainers had brought from the grocery store and climbed into the bus—now converted to an oven by the afternoon sun.

Sitting on the bus eating ice chips out of a filthy helmet—a gummy plastic bowl with a slimy film of sweat and blood inside—I looked out at the bank sign which read "95 Degrees." For reasons I cannot begin to understand, that instant became one of the permanent and profound portraits on the wall of my otherwise feeble memory. It is a clear picture on the gallery of my mind, framed next to the bum on the train.

With the picture of the bank sign I remember the heat, the pain, and the fatigue of those days. I remember the humiliation of having the kid outrun me at the last second. I remember the absolute lack of concern about how dirty my helmet was as I sucked on the ice chips melting in the smelly plastic bowl. I remember the starkness of the transition from harvesting to football. Four days earlier I double-clutched a two-ton Ford to crawl out of a field up onto the gravel road.

Today I lined up on the goal line with the other backs and ends to run one-hundred-yard wind sprints. Four days earlier I was inside a clogged-up combine jerking straw from the feeder chain. Today I was inside a heated yellow bus. Four days earlier I ate greasy meals in Shelby, Montana. Today I ate ice chips out of a helmet. Four days ago I read about the Dempsey-Gibbons fight—again—on a placemat. Today I read the bank sign. Four days earlier I was a shaggy, unsupervised kid on the adventure of his life. Today I was a bald, heavily-supervised kid in the pain of his life.

The gap between those two worlds felt huge. From freedom to constraint. From responsibility to domination. From pool hopping to homework. From wheatie to high school kid. It was changing gears without double-clutching and some of the gear teeth grinding off and chipping around in the bottom of the gear box.

The gap felt too wide to cross in three short days in an aluminum canoe and my Dad's yellow station wagon. For a few days it felt like I had lost my mind and that neither place was real—my second mild case of culture shock in three months.

My senior year was basically good except that Kristy Barnes dumped me after the prom, and we lost the district final in basketball when our cross-town rivals threw in a half-court blind, off-balance, no-look, prayer of a shot.

In the spring the US Forest Service transferred my Dad to Tucson, Arizona, and the family was slated to move the day after I graduated from high school in June.

By this time I had no interest in going back to harvesting with Don. It was not that I had a bad experience or any fear about another summer. Tucson seemed like a greater adventure than something I had already experienced. I wrote a letter to Don telling him that I was moving with my family to Arizona and subtly implying that my parents were expecting me to come along—which was not true. Not that they had any problem with me moving to Arizona with them, but they would have been fine with me going back to harvesting.

I didn't hear back from Don, but I figured I had done my duty to inform him.

We got up early the day after my graduation. Having already said goodbye to folks at the Job Corps Center, we simply loaded the last things in the yellow Bronco and the yellow Ford station wagon and hit the road. It would take us two days to get to Tucson.

I had a cashiers' check for $500 in my wallet. I had spent the other $250 on I cannot remember what. I would spend the $500 on my first semester at the University of Arizona. The memories would outlive the money by decades.

My dad let me drive the Bronco much of the way. The station wagon was ahead of us. The rag top on the Bronco flapped incessantly. The Black Hills were getting smaller and smaller in my rearview mirror. I was reminded of my severe homesickness when those same hills got smaller as we pulled out with the harvest crew on our way to Montana. Now it was not homesickness it was just surreal.

As we had done every two to three years our family pulled up stakes and moved. Every time it felt strange and every time I felt like I was moving away from some place that was fictional and to another place that was fictional—suffering some sort of psychological disconnection from reality and from myself. I again withdrew into the emotional numbness to dull the pain of always leaving friends and always being the new kid and knowing that it was only going to happen again.

As distant as my summer of wheat harvesting already felt those ninety days had clearly lodged in my memory and my psyche.

EPILOGUE 2013: DIESEL FUMES

Someone was with me.

Forty six years have gone away like diesel fumes rising off a blistering Nebraska wheat field.

I am 61. I am fighting my way home on a commute up a very busy, 6-lane Texas surface road.

I have written Wheatie. I had it professionally edited by a very skilled woman. I am half-way through my rewrites based on her insights. After these four and a half decades I am closing in on the completion of a cherished project. The story and summer of Wheatie are very much on my mind.

The drive from my office to home is 12 miles due north on Custer Avenue. I know it well. I know where it pinches down to two lanes and where the school zone is and where the three-quarters mark is and where the worst pot holes are and where the camera monitored stop lights are. I know how bad the traffic will be if I leave at any given time. Tonight I have left my office at approximately the worst time for traffic. Traffic is heavy and commuters are tense and anxious, but I am not.

Tonight I am not joining the fray. Tonight I am content. I am not weaving in and out of lanes. I am not tailgating. I am not running yellow lights. I am listening to The Brothers Karamazov on audio book and I am lost in an exceedingly sad and evil story set in Russia of decades past.

Allyosha is grieving the death of his beloved mentor Father Zosima and I get caught at a light. I am maybe 5 or 7 cars back in the pack and the line of cars in my rearview mirror is three times that long. The light changes and the line accordions forward. Now we are up to speed. On my right I see a wheat field sandwiched between subdivisions and a combine running and ripe wheat being pulled into the throat of a massive John Deere.

I hesitate on my idea for only one second and then I brake, signal, exit the speeding commuters, and jump the curb up into the wheat field. Parking 20 feet into the stubble I hurry out, take out my phone and begin to video the beautiful obnoxiously noisy machine. The sight of the combine in ripe wheat and the smell of the diesel fumes and the heat of the field flood over me—it is 1969.

What happens in the psyche of a boy in these formative adventures like my wheatie summer? What happens that to lodge so deeply in him all of the memory and fear and excitement and discovery and sadness and simple awe of living and then flashes it up so vividly?

I walked toward the combine. I partly wanted a ride but I partly wanted to tell someone who would understand—to tell him that I had driven one of these in the summer of 1969 and that I had hauled wheat to the elevators and that I had suffered the heat and itching of the summer. I wanted to tell someone who understood and therefore who would welcome me, an aging white-collar commuter, into his circle and his confidence and would respect me for having done something substantial on the earth.

As I got near, the combine slowed and then stopped. The smell of diesel washed over me. I could see a fiftyish man with a dirty round face leaning over to open the door. He shut down the machine and looked down at me out of the open door of the cab.

In a kind and curious voice he said, "Can I help you?" though he must have been thinking, "What kind of a suburban clown has driven his car up into the field and walked out here?"

"I drove one of these when I was a kid and I just wanted to see one again," I answered.

He apparently knew what was going on in me and immediately asked, "Do you want to ride?"

"I would love to!"

I climbed up the ladder and into an air-conditioned cab and pulled the door shut behind me. The driver's name was Tommy and we rode around in huge squares with the corners cut off while we got each other's names and stories. We talked about harvesting and combines and heat and God and family and money troubles. We talked about my book and how he wanted to read it and how I promised to give him a copy once we were Facebook friends. We talked about how combines had changed and who owned this machine and what he did when the wheat was not ripe.

Then we were silent. We fell under the familiar rhythmic spell of the turning fan and the reciprocating cutter bar and the roar of a diesel engine and the unrelenting jarring of the beautiful, complex, threshing machine. We watched mesmerized like campers staring at a campfire. We just rode round and round and Tommy ran the monster skillfully. I was in the club and happy.

My head filled up with, "In-A-Gadda-Da-Vida baby, don't you know that I love you?" Kerry was grinning at me out the window of his Camaro. I saw Mark on his knees in the stubble leaning hard on a long wrench. Don was standing in the trailer house kitchen holding out his sweat soaked shirt to a very angry wife who pretended not to see it. A moaning driver lay writhing in the very middle of a mound of wheat. Carrie waved at me that dismissive wave out the window of an old sedan. My dad said, "I'd keep your duffle bag locked when you are not with it."

It was all vivid and just as it had been. But I was different. There was a calm in me that had been born and begun to grow very slowly sometime in that anxious summer. Life was no longer an endless series of fears and fretting. My problems were bigger and my fears were smaller. The unknowns were not terrifying, or even particularly bothersome. The intense anxiety that accompanied almost every piece of my harvest summer had mellowed into calm, that though not the epitome of peace was certainly a very enjoyable state by comparison.

At one level this new calm could be explained by having more resources, more experience and more personal power of one kind or another. But at a more primal level the calm was a change at the soul-molecular level. Something was different, more mature. Something was clearer about reality and more confident of wellbeing. Someone was with me. Some perspective had entered in.

There was also born in me that distant summer a seed that grew into an easy comfort with people who were different than me. In 1969 Carrie and the older wheaties and Dan and Marie and angry farmers and beautiful girls all threatened me. Now, I had eaten supper in African homes with people to whom I could not speak. Engaged 12-year olds on airplanes. Sat comfortably in Gypsie churches in Slovakia. Been one of three white faces in a high-school gathering of more than six hundred people in Liberia. Taught through translators in 12 or 14 countries. Eaten muktuk in an Eskimo village. Struck up friendly conversations with Jews and Muslims and Hindus and on and on. Today I sat next to Tommy with an easy friendliness.

The willingness to take risks, so rewarded that sixteenth summer of my life, was more alive than ever. The spark that pulled me to respond to a "travel required" job also pulled me to hop a curb and drive into a wheat field and walk up to a combine. It had pulled me into work that took me to dozens of countries around the world. "Travel Required." It had motivated me to quit a great job at 60 to tackle another job that was far more "shaky."

I had also in that few months been gripped by the sadness of so many lives, by the deep sadness of so many relationships. In that summer I had a front row seat on 38 year old men who had no education, no moral compass, no sense of responsibility, no direction, no certainty about how many children they had, and no money to put gas in their car. That first exposure to people living on the edge or already over the edge bred contempt in me. The contempt certainly grew out of the immaturity and arrogance of my youth rather than out of the nature of their lives. These years later my contempt has turned to compassion, a tainted compassion to be sure but at least compassion.

In that summer, I also had a front row seat on a marriage that was a fountain of sadness for a woman. Her husband was apparently happy to chase other women when he was out of her sight and was also mostly oblivious to the pain he caused her in that. He seemed unconcerned with the pain that he caused by most all aspects of his relational style.

Now with my commute unexpectedly interrupted I thought about her as I was jostling around in the wonderful memory squares in this wheat field beside my commute. I thought about her confused mixture of sadness, anger, sense of betrayal and sense of entitlement. I thought about her death in a car accident the summer after I was a wheatie.

About how her sad, disillusioned life ended at the intersection of two dirt roads deep in wheat country. It was country that she hated. And she had the sadness of dying in it. I thought about a station wagon on its top with the tires still spinning and potato salad sprayed out the back window and a blood covered dead woman with the life gone out of her but the sadness not. I wondered what Don had felt at her death and what had become of her children. And I felt deep sadness for her and for Don and for the children.

That sadness was in me more than ever now. It was better managed as sadness management goes but it was also much deeper. Now it was a sadness grounded not only in watching people I barely knew but in personal pain and in having a front row seat on the sadness of people I love.

Somewhere in the emotional and moral wrestling of that summer I had become aware of a diametric divide in the choices before me. I lost some of my naiveté and gained some courage. I lost some provincial perspective and gained a greater sense of the outside world.

And somewhere there was born in me that summer a desire to live my life well. I had no idea what this meant. Today I would call it integrity. Then I mostly saw what I did not want.

This much I decided that summer. I decided that I wanted to do all I could to stay with my wife and to cherish her—knowing that it might be beyond my control someday. I decided I wanted to know and love and live with and care for my children—if it were at all in my power. I decided I wanted to apologize for the relational sins in me. I decided I wanted to live above personal addiction and the tyranny of my own desires if I could. I decided I wanted to tell the truth and stop being so incessantly deceptive. I decided I wanted to be honest if I could.

All of these I have done to a degree—to a failing degree at times— but I am still fighting for this road in life. Much as I have failed, I love integrity more than ever and that love was nurtured in my wheatie summer. So much of what I experienced that summer was a Peter Rabbit cautionary tale—but without the soft, beautiful, colorful illustrations and without the happy ending. I took it to heart.

All that was germinated and grew in me in that summer and all that grew in me was not of me. I am clear on that. If I am sure of anything today it is that God was in the middle of that hot and dusty summer.

There was much that formed me and impressed me in the summer of 1969. In that summer I voluntarily threw myself into an adventure. That adventure then took me, involuntarily, into so much that was new or dangerous or unknown or surreal.

It always strikes me, these decades later, that I remember so much about my short career as a wheatie. In general, my memory is horrible and an ongoing handicap to me. But from that summer I remember so many people and so many emotions and so many places and so many incidents and so many smells and so many images. So much is not only retained in my memory but retained vividly in my memory.

Don Dexter and his custom harvesting crew took me so far out of my comfort zones that I paid attention to everything and registered everything and thought about everything and remembered an amazing amount.

The aggregate experience of that dry, hot, chaff-filled summer imprinted me. I think it was for the good. Homesick and miserable as I made myself for much of the summer, I look back on those months with terrific fondness.

Tommy turned the corner and the header dipped too deep taking a little divot and jolting the machine. I woke up in 2013. It was a good place to be.

I thanked Tommy profusely for my ride and climbed down from the shaking metal perch. He waved and moved forward into the standing wheat.

The diesel fumes were thick and wonderful. I backed away and stood for a time in the stubble. The John Deere turned away from me spitting straw out her tail.

There is still travel required for me. Tomorrow I leave for Morocco. But today I turned back to my car and my commute and The Brothers Karamazov and to my wife of 39 years waiting just 5 miles away.

There is a break in the traffic as it is held at bay by the light. I jump the curb back onto the street. I get up to speed and ease north toward home.

Shelby, Montana. Casa Blanca, Morocco. Travel Required.

ABOUT THE AUTHOR

Dave Gibson began his life in He Dog, South Dakota and grew up as the son of a US Forest Ranger and a pioneer prairie woman. He lived in South Dakota (three different times), Texas, California, Wyoming, Colorado, and Arizona before going to college in Montana. His "career path" has been exceedingly crooked and has included retail sales, forestry, freight loading, college teaching, college administration, and executive leadership in three different companies. Along the way he earned a bachelor's, a master's, and a doctorate in three different fields of study.

Dave has been married to Kathi 42 years; they are blessed with three married children and eight grandchildren. These 15 people are the joy of his life.

The "travel required" piece of the Wheatie summer has continued to be an important part of Dave's life. To date he has visited 49 states (he needs to get to West Virginia), 31 countries, and five continents. That travel has included walking, backpacking, hitchhiking, skateboards, tricycles, bicycles, cross-country skis, downhill skis, snowshoes, cars, trucks, combines, planes, helicopters, boats, trains, The Chunnel, buses, rickshaws, motorized rickshaws, jeepneys, subways, motorcycles, tramways, T bars, rope tows, jet skis, ferries, elevated rails, all-terrain vehicles, track vehicles, cog railways, shuttle busses, toboggans, sleds, dune buggies, and his beloved, now deceased, 1962 Dodge Town and Country Power Wagon.

Since 1971, two years after the harvest summer, Dave has been a sold out and deeply grateful follower of Jesus.

32449855R00121

Made in the USA
Middletown, DE
04 June 2016